MW01536137

UNELECTABLE

U̶N̶ELECTABLE

MAKING SPACE FOR A FUTURE
WITH FEMALE LEADERS

LUCY WHICHELO

NDP

NEW DEGREE PRESS

COPYRIGHT © 2021 LUCY WHICHELO

All rights reserved.

UNELECTABLE

Making Space for a Future With Female Leaders

ISBN	978-1-63676-863-2	*Paperback*
	978-1-63730-179-1	*Kindle Ebook*
	978-1-63730-307-8	*Ebook*

To the staff and students at Elmwood School for Girls, and
to my new friends at McGill Women in Leadership

To Adrienne

Enjoy your copy

— Wapi

TABLE OF CONTENTS

––––––

INTRODUCTION

———

The outbreak of the COVID-19 pandemic in Wuhan, China, and its worldwide spread throughout 2020 and into 2021, has taken the world and flipped it upside down. In addition to worldwide climate change, rapid advancement of technologies, and the simultaneous conflicts of overpopulation and aging population, COVID-19 is pushing us into a new era of global leadership and it looks like it might finally be a female-friendly one.

Since the beginning of the ongoing coronavirus pandemic, it has become apparent female-led countries have fared better in handling the pandemic. The effectiveness of Denmark, Finland, Germany, Iceland, Norway, Taiwan, and New Zealand—all nations with female heads of state—are cited by media outlets as supporting evidence that women are indeed capable and powerful leaders. The BBC, for example, acknowledged Jacinda Arden's leadership in New Zealand as "a model response of empathy, clarity and trust in science," and *The Guardian* noted Angela Merkel's "proactive and coordinated policy response" which left Germany far better off than its European neighbors in terms of COVID-19 cases and deaths.[1,2] Some even claim they are perhaps even better than their male counterparts. This positive and celebratory commentary, however, is certainly a new phenomenon for female politicians.

Given that women only make up about 10 percent of national leaders, they are still so unusual that they tend to stand out and draw a lot of scrutiny. The fact that women are finally starting to be seen as important and capable leaders is a great sign of progress, and I believe it points toward a new age of inclusivity for female leaders. I have great hope the women and girls of the future will be able to look at the world around them and think, "I can be prime minister, too."

When I was younger, I wanted to be prime minister. I may also have wanted to be a ballerina, an astronaut, and a novelist, but the point is I believed I could do any of those things easily if I put my mind to it. As a child, I was surrounded by positive female and male role models who encouraged these beliefs. In particular, during my high school years at Elmwood School for Girls I was surrounded by people who encouraged my peers and I to pursue our career goals and passions. I never thought I was less competent than my male counterparts or felt I wasn't suitable for a position because of my gender. I feel grateful for the confidence my experience at Elmwood has instilled, as it has helped dispel some of the less encouraging narratives that I have become

1   "Coronavirus: How New Zealand Relied on Science and Empathy" *BBC News*, April 20, 2020.

2   Jon Henley, "Female-Led Countries Handled Coronavirus Better, Study Suggests" *The Guardian*, August 18, 2020.

increasingly exposed to throughout my working and university experiences.

As I started to venture out of those sheltered walls of my home and of my school, however, I started to see the world in a slightly different way; you could say my rose-tinted glasses were slipping off. As a student studying political science, it has become my job to stay informed about the things going on outside my own personal bubble and in the world around me. Inevitably, this has meant that I have tuned in to some of the less encouraging and pessimistic stories out there. The conversations I see and hear in the classroom, on social media, and on the news are still wrought with misogynistic undertones, ones which see feminine traits as less desirable but also see women without feminine traits as less desirable—a double-edged sword, so to speak. I think it is exactly this kind of environment that discourages women from pursuing leadership positions. These double standards and double binds certainly hold women back when it comes to finding success in politics. No wonder women seem to be so unelectable!

Female politicians of the past and present have endured many struggles when it comes to trying for, and being in, political leadership positions, and our society still seems to be uncomfortable with the idea of women being in positions of power. All we have to do is turn to statistics to see it. UN Women estimates that globally men represent 77 percent of parliamentarians, 82 percent of government ministers, 93 percent of heads of government, and 94 percent of heads of state.[3] Today, one can name all of the current female country leaders in less than thirty seconds; currently, only nineteen out of 193 countries have a female head of state or government. We can also turn and look at the treatment of female leaders in the media and in the press. Harsh criticisms surrounding women's appearance, voice, personality, values, capability, and fulfillment as wives and mothers run rampant and to a much greater extent than experienced by males. After seeing these prejudices and biases against women unfold around me, my childhood dream of becoming prime minister has certainly become less appetizing.

That being said, while I have become aware of all of the double binds and double standards and daunting challenges women in politics are facing, I believe it is possible to find a way to push back on these prejudices and look toward creating space for a brighter future for female leaders. Positive changes are already well on their way, and in 2020 we are at a place women could have only dreamed about even just twenty years ago. We are seeing a greater willingness of society to have a more open, honest and vulnerable conversation about these struggles, and we are starting to see society actively try and change the way we think about and treat women in politics through the means of education, ads, social media, female role models, and allies. The success and support for the female pandemic power players, like Jacinda Arden and Angela Merkel mentioned earlier, certainly point to this.

---

3   "Facts and Figures: Women's Leadership and Political Participation" *UN Women*, accessed January 19, 2020.

So, while the first part of my book will walk through double binds, double standards, and challenges that act as a barrier to women in their political careers, the second part of my book will show how I see things changing for the better, and the third part will walk through the steps we can take as a society to continue this progress. Through this "debunking" of the close-minded and exclusive concepts of gender and leadership that have been reinforced for centuries, I believe we will be able to overcome this paradox still hindering female leaders. I have confidence that women of the future *will* be electable, as long as we continue to address and work on changing our beliefs and attitudes about gender and leadership through these conversations.

In writing this book I hope I can be part of this conversation and, through my own personal research, conversations, and self-reflections, contribute to this critical debunking process. I also hope this book will provide a vision for a way forward in creating a space for a female-led future. While I want this book to encourage you to look inwards, to recognize your subconscious preconceptions and biases, to think about where you come from and why you think the way you do (even if it is a little uncomfortable), I also want you to look outward and look to one another to talk, listen, learn, support, and act on this issue.

So, if you are an aspiring female leader, know an aspiring female leader, or just want to see women being given an equal chance to be one for a change, then this book is for you. Read it in order or out of order, read it all at once or flip through it when you have a break, take notes, pass it around to friends, share its stories and its message, and share what you think about them with others. Get the conversation going. It is by doing this that women can finally be seen as electable.

PART 1:

THE GENDERED CATCH-22

INTRODUCTION

Joseph Heller's infamous 1961 novel *Catch-22* tells of the absurd bureaucratic and paradoxical constraints on soldiers in World War II. It follows the life of antihero Captain John Yossarian in World War II while he struggles against the rules of the military system which are inaccessible to and slanted against those lower in the hierarchy.[4] Over fifty years later, the book may be more relevant than ever, especially when it comes to talking about the pressures women face in politics. A catch-22 is a paradoxical situation from which an individual cannot escape because of contradictory rules or limitations. Being unable to get a job without experience but being unable to get experience without a job is one example. Being a woman in a position of political leadership is another.

When people think of leaders and leadership qualities, they think of them in stereotypically masculine terms. Research conducted by New York University professors Andrea Vial and Jaime Napier and published by the *Frontiers in Psychology* journal in October 2018 found traditionally feminine

---

4   Joseph Heller, *Catch-22: a novel*, (New York: The Modern library, 1961)

traits such as intuition and empathy were valued less in leaders in comparison to more masculine traits such as competence and assertiveness.[5] As a result, for women to succeed they are expected to act more stereotypically masculine. The problem with this, however, is when a woman does not fit the role traditionally assigned to her and attempts to claim a traditionally male position she is seen as breaking the norm, and, as we will see in the coming chapters, will typically suffer negative consequences as a result. This is the problem of "likability." Women who are not assertive and fit the gender stereotype of traditional femininity in being gentle and "pretty" are liked more but are not considered as leadership material, while women who reject those qualities are labelled as "bitchy," unfeminine, and aggressive, and hence generally disliked. In both cases, women are then less likely to be promoted into a leadership position than their male counterpart. More simply put, they're dealing with a catch-22.

This double bind for female leaders makes it hard to be successful in the realm of politics, an area already riddled with intense pressure, scrutiny, and competition. For the same kind of leadership behavior, women might be penalized while a man is commended. No matter what a woman does, whether she be assertive and forceful or gentle and empathetic, she becomes problematic. When we look around the world and wonder why women still seem to be so damn unelectable, it really comes down to this: if we want to make the world a more welcoming space for women leaders, we must first debunk the paradox of gender and of leadership

---

5   Andrea Vial and Jaime L. Napier, "Unnecessary Frills: Communality as a Nice (But Expendable) Trait in Leaders" *Frontiers in Psychology* 9 (2018): 1866.

that has been reinforced for centuries to overcome this paradox and create a future that welcomes female electability.

In this section, I hope I can be part of this debunking process. The upcoming chapters in the first part of this book will take a look at a variety of examples of impossible and unfair standards women in politics are held to, from the way they dress, to the way the parent, to the way they talk, sound, and act. To highlight this catch-22 phenomenon, each chapter covers a different standard, with many of them directly contrasting those covered in the adjacent chapters. As a result, it may make most sense to read these chapters chronologically. Buckle up—and maybe keep a stress ball on hand for the really frustrating parts!

CHAPTER 1:

IN-STYLE

———

As a young girl, my parents always told me if you judge a book by its cover, you will miss a great story. When we are children, we are taught to look beyond what's on the outside and to focus on what's on the inside. This lesson, however, seems to have gone down the drain when it comes to judging our politicians, especially our female ones.

Jeannette Rankin, the first women member of Congress, was elected to the House of Representatives in 1916. *The Washington Post* published an article titled "Congresswoman Rankin Real Girl: Likes Nice Gowns and Tidy Hair" describing her as, "thoroughly feminine—from her charmingly coiffed swirl of chestnut hair to the small, high and distinctively French heels. She is given to soft and clinging gowns, and, according to her own confession, is very fond of moving pictures."[6] Rankin's clothes and hairstyle became the main topic of conversation and she was exposed to some rather tactless scrutiny and examination over her dress and appearance before

---

6   "Masquerading as Miss Rankin" *US House of Representatives: History, Art & Archives*" 2017, accessed January 27, 2021.

she could even have a chance to establish a track record of legislation or convey any of her political ideals. According to the House's History, Art, & Archives website, the article was typical of coverage of early congresswomen, whose looks and dress often received outsized attention.[7] Whether the appearance-focused reports stemmed from the fact reporters had, until that point, only known women as a society page subject, or were, more insidiously, an attempt to delegitimize the inclusion of women in Congress, we will never know. But what we do know is this was just the beginning of the long and winding road of media reports on clothes and shoes and hair constituting a woman's identity as related to her appearance.

From Hillary Clinton to Sarah Palin (whose examples will be discussed later in the upcoming chapters), women who hold public office are too often analyzed, judged, and criticized for their appearance. Articles and news coverage on the clothes, hair, and sexuality of female politicians somehow manage to pass as political journalism when they should really be placed in the pages of an *InStyle* magazine, and oftentimes receive more attention, and therefore more influence, than media that actually reports on the women's political platforms and perspectives. As a staff writer at my university's political journal, I often have to catch myself from reproducing these shallow and materialistic reporting tendencies in my own work. When I do my research for my articles, I check my information with multiple media outlets and news sites. I have found the stereotyping and criticism of female politician's appearance and dress is a common theme among

---

7   *Ibid.*

all of them. When you see so much of that kind of content around you, it takes conscious effort to push that kind of thinking out of your subconscious analyses. I certainly have to check myself to make sure I don't end up joining in on the criticism bandwagon. I think it's a shame others aren't putting in as much effort to do the same as well.

As a result of our society's increasingly poor journalistic standards, women end up being obliged to seek approval of their electorates not on the basis of their competence, but on the basis of their looks. It seems rather shameful to think we still live in a world that cares more about how a woman looks then what she thinks. So when it comes to talking about women in positions of power, the media and the public instead fall back on what they are comfortable with: critiquing women's appearance. All of this goes to show how people are still uncomfortable with the concept of women rejecting traditional roles and taking up positions of power; the media's obsession with women's appearance and dress are a symptom of something bigger. Women still aren't completely welcome in the halls of government.

In light of all of this, it is a wonder people are so surprised to find out only nineteen out of 193 countries have a female head of state or government, or that women still only make up 24.3 percent of national parliaments.[8] Sure, there may not be official barriers that say "no female leaders" or "women not welcome in parliament," but there doesn't need to be. The misogynistic media coverage and treatment women receive

---

8   "Facts and Figures: Women's Leadership and Political Participation" *UN Women,* accessed January 27, 2020.

in the workplace is enough to push women out of politics. The stereotyping, sexualization, and general gendered discrimination of female politicians teaches us success is only attainable for those who match society's narrow definition of femininity, beauty, and sexuality, and this ultimately puts women off of their political aspirations and careers. I know I would certainly be hesitant to sign up for a career in which I am constantly critiqued for what I wear and how I look, and I'm sure I'm not the only one.

I talked to one of my close friends and colleagues at McGill University to see if my apprehension of such a career in politics had some company. Louise Hoffman and I have been studying political science and communications together at McGill University since 2017. In fact, Louise was the first friend I made at university, and we have helped each other maneuver through our academic careers and political aspirations ever since. Since Louise and I have both been geared toward careers in the political field for a while now, it has been interesting to see how our thoughts and feelings about being a woman in politics have changed. In talking to Louise, we both agreed the appearance-based scrutiny we see women face in the political sphere is a sizeable turn-off when it comes to considering careers of our own. The expectations of dress for women in politics and the constant critique of women's appearance by the media has been designed to make women uncomfortable. "For me," Louise said, "being uncomfortable is certainly not conducive to good work, but rather to insecurity and doubt, feelings I do not want to have accentuated when entering a career." Furthermore, she noted that the beauty standards women in politics are held to typically presume a certain body type (white, young, slim) and requires money and labour (eating healthy, going to the gym, getting your hair done, etc.) which "takes away from political work and disadvantages women when compared to their male counterparts." To Louise, this was all made very clear by the critical media coverage seen in Hillary Clinton's Presidential Campaign as well as Alexandra Ocasio Cortez's *Vanity Fair* cover, which highlights the way in which "it seems women in politics cannot do anything right when it comes to their appearance." For her, this is "a challenge I do not feel like facing...I would rather stay away from the spotlight and scrutiny that comes with most (high-profile) political careers."

As Louise and I have ultimately come to recognize, a career as a woman in politics is one that is bound to be tied with unfair standards and scrutinizing of our appearance. It is recognition like this that plays a part in pushing many women away from political careers. A 2019 research study done by Amanda Haraldsson and Lena Wängnerud on "the effect of media sexism on women's political ambition: evidence from a worldwide study" found a negative relationship between media sexism and the share of candidates for the lower chamber of national parliaments who are women.[9] The researchers looked at data on media sexism from the Global Media Monitoring Project and data on the share of female political candidates from the Inter-Parliamentary Union. The study found nascent political ambition is less likely to develop among women where media sexism is high, and those women who are politically ambitious will be less likely to express this ambition by becoming a candidate than

---

9   Amanda Haraldsson and Lena Wängnerud, "The Effect of Media Sexism on Women's Political Ambition: Evidence from a Worldwide Study" *Feminist Media Studies* 19, no. 4 (May 19, 2019): 525–41.

they would have been in an environment free from media sexism. These results suggest sexist portrayals of women in the media stifle ambition among women who, in a less sexist media environment, would be willing to stand as political candidates.

Unfortunately, however, our political discourse still tends to place the onus on women when it comes to dealing with the underrepresentation of women in politics and treats the issue as though it is a result of women's choice, as if women simply opt out of politics because of a biological predisposition that makes them uninterested or unqualified. I'm no doctor, but I don't think a woman's biology is so different than a man's to make women completely reject any capacity that isn't a domestic one. The conversation hinges on blaming women for opting out and shying away from leadership positions without paying attention to the reasons why women opt out and shy away in the first place. The reasons why over-whelming numbers of women are opting out are not just coincidences or one offs in women's personal decisions, they are a result of societal conditions created by everyone, not just women. Because of this, nothing will change if we settle with a "that's just the way things are" kind of attitude. We need to be curious. We need to uncover those reasons why women are opting out, and we need to address them and hold everyone accountable when it comes to doing so.

CHAPTER 2:

THE PANTSUIT

———

Hillary Clinton is undeniably the "Queen of Pantsuits." They are bright orange or teal or black, grey, and white. Sometimes her jackets have round collars, other times half collars, and every now and then a silk scarf is thrown in on special occasions. She even wore one in her official First Lady portrait in 2003, breaking the longtime tradition of ballgowns and pearls. The "Hillary Clinton Pantsuit Phenomenon" is a well-known one. Clinton's penchant for pantsuits is so well known it has produced memes, *Saturday Night Live* jokes, and even Halloween costumes available for purchase on Amazon.

To avoid the fashion-focused reports and critiques that previously mentioned Jeannette Rankin, and other female politicians had received before her, the simple uniform of loose-fitting, monochromatic colored pantsuits seemed like the right decision for Clinton when it came to her 2016 campaign wardrobe. Pantsuits are practical and comfortable (two things women's clothing historically haven't been), while also being professional and put together. For Hillary, the pantsuits were supposed to work as an anti-distraction technique. "Since there wasn't much to say or report on what

I wore," she thought, "maybe people would focus on what I was saying instead," Clinton writes in her autobiography *What Happened*.[10] In the autobiography, Clinton writes she thought "it would be good to do what male politicians do and wear more or less the same thing every day." As a woman running for president, Hillary thought her pantsuits would act as a kind of visual cue; if she could dress the way her male counterparts did, perhaps they (and others) would see her more as an equal. The idea that dressing like a man would afford women more respect has not been an uncommon one. Nineteenth-century abolitionist, women's rights advocate, and journalist Jane Grey Cannon Swisshelm reflected on the belief "that masculine supremacy lay in the form of their garments, and that a woman dressed like a man would be as potent as he." In light of all these things, it makes sense Hillary would think wearing a pantsuit would be the best way to get around gendered stereotypes and judgments surrounding her code of dress.

Sometimes, however, things don't always make sense.

In her attempt to be taken more seriously, Hillary was punished for not conforming to societal gender expectations and codes of dress. Though early celebrity adopters of the pantsuit such as Marlene Dietrich and Katharine Hepburn fought the stereotypes women were either too sensual to hide their bodies under men's clothes or that the clothes were a symptom of women being too masculine as individuals, the anti-pantsuit sentiment prevailed. "Hideous," "unflattering,"

---

10   Hillary Rodham Clinton, *What Happened*, (New York: Simon & Schuster, 2017)

and "unfeminine" were the words used by the media outlets when commenting on her pantsuit. Twitter discussions
and YouTube videos made about Hillary Clinton being tired,
overweight, and grandmother-ish gained popularity and
took hold of political conversations and debates. Even *Project Runway*'s Tim Gunn joined in, saying in 2011, "Why must
she dress that way? I think she's confused about her gender."[11]
While Gunn followed his statement by saying, "I have great
respect for her intellect and her tenacity and for what she
does for our country in her governmental role... I just wish
she could send a stronger message about American fashion," it doesn't change the fact when it comes to evaluating
female leaders, our world seems to care more about their style
choices than anything else, and we are quick to punish those
who don't put the required amount of grooming time in. To
be fair, the media has also taken some significant attacks
on Donald Trump's hair (perhaps another symptom of our
patriarchal obsessions with manhood and virility), but the
criticism male politicians receive for their looks miniscule
relative to the criticism women receive for theirs.

Unlike Tim Gunn, and numerous other media coverage and
news outlets, I don't care what either of them wear. Opposed
to her politics or not, Hillary Clinton is a capable and experienced political leader and she should be treated as such. What
she does or doesn't wear is not relevant and shouldn't matter
when it comes to judging her as a political leader. Instead of
discussing fashion choices, a more productive focus would be
on discussing our leaders' positions on universal healthcare

---

11   Karin Tanabe, "Tim Gunn Still Hates Hillary Clinton's Pantsuits"
     POLITICO, July 8, 2011

or views on taxing the wealthy. These would certainly be more productive questions than "what inspired your outfit today?"

In light of all this, however, the pantsuit has managed to become a power symbol and a rallying cry for female empowerment. In the months leading up to the 2016 presidential election, Beyoncé and her backup dancers donned pantsuit costumes during a pro-Clinton concert, and a flash mob popped up in New York City's Union Square dancing to a Justin Timberlake song in the Clinton-style attire as a show of support for the democratic candidate.[12] Pantsuit Nation, the secret group on Facebook for Clinton supporters, is another example of women reclaiming the symbol of the pantsuit as a feminist one, and using it to unite those to fight against the patriarchy. The page has allowed Hillary Clinton to embrace the jokes made about her pantsuits, turning criticism into a conversation about how the dissection of women's appearances and bodies is still a key issue in today's presidential races. In this way, one might see the pantsuit controversy as having actually been a helpful one in directing us to a future of dress codes that don't reduce women to their gender identity.

If "feminine" is what the people want, however, maybe politicians would benefit from dropping the pantsuits in favor of more form-fitting dresses, high heels, blonde highlights, and hair extensions? Wrong. While it is the case that wearing a pantsuit fails to send a "strong message about American

---

12   Deirdre Clemente, "A President in a Pantsuit?" *APNews*, November 7, 2016

fashion," being well dressed doesn't seem to be helping female politicians out either. Sarah Palin is an excellent example of this.

During her 2008 candidacy for vice president for the Republican Party, Sarah Palin leaped into notoriety. However, few aspects of her candidacy received more attention than her wardrobe choices and her sex appeal. Rather than be criticized for looking dowdy or wearing masculine pantsuits like Clinton, Palin instead took flack for her campaign stylist going on a $150,000 shopping spree to make sure Palin would look the part, and then received criticism about how dressing "in such a bold manner," showed she was "someone who has come to steal the spotlight rather than share it."[13] Fox News chief Roger Ailes admitted he only hired Sarah Palin as a paid contributor "because she was hot and got ratings," and a music video entitled "Red, White and MILF" (short for "Mom I'd like to f*ck") has appeared all over the internet, awarding Palin the honored title of "the sexiest politician in the US."[14] It is interesting to see Palin was polarizing, not because she insinuated Barack Obama was a terrorist or because of her anti-abortion, anti-gay agenda, but because she was "hot." MSNBC analyst Donny Deutsch told *Morning Joe* viewers we shouldn't be surprised Mrs. Palin divided the nation because "this is the first woman in power with sexual appeal...We're used to seeing a woman in power as non-threatening." Whether or not she was competent, however, Deutsch told CNBC: "It doesn't matter...I want her

---

13   Robin Givhan, "Did You Notice Sarah Palin's Sweater? Good. You Were Supposed to" *The Washington Post,* January 20, 2016

14   Jennifer Pozner, "Hot And Bothering: Media Treatment Of Sarah Palin" *NPR.org,* July 8, 2009

laying next to me in bed. That's the way people vote."[15] (After a comment like that it shouldn't be a surprise Deutsch also told his viewers Hillary Clinton lost because "she didn't put a skirt on!")

So as it stands, if you're underdressed, you're frumpy, but if you're too dolled up you're shallow and unintelligent. If you're unattractive or overweight, you'll be ignored, but if you're pretty or have sex appeal, you're suspected of getting by on your looks. If you don't spend time and money on your appearance, you're gauche, but if you do you're vain. Women just can't seem to get it right, can they?

These impossibly perfect standards put an immense pressure on women, teens, and even young girls to constantly look just right. As a young girl one of my favorite movies was *The Princess Diaries*. The movie's most well-known scene, and my own personal favorite as a child, was her princess make-over scene. Mia Thermopolis, played by Anne Hathaway, was turned from an unpopular, frizzy-haired and awkward-looking high school girl into a full-blown princess with new hair, clothes, jewelry, and makeup to fulfill her role as princess of Genovia. As the story continues, Mia's best friend is taken over by the green-eyed monster of jealousy and leaves her for having changed too much and shames her for caring about her appearance. This shows how, even in a kid's movie, we create narratives that perpetuate the idea you need to be pretty to have confidence, friends, popularity, and love interests, but you can't be too pretty or try too hard otherwise, you'll look vain and alienate your friends. This storyline is a

15   *Ibid.*

common one, from Tai's sexed-up transformation in *Clueless*, to Cady's popularity project in *Mean Girls*, to Laney Boggs' prom queen metamorphosis in *She's All That*. After repeatedly watching characters in movies like these get made over again and again, it's no wonder girls and women, myself included, feel pressure to edit their appearance to get their appearance "just right" to fit in.

Bay Buchanan's book *The Extreme Makeover of Hillary (Rodham) Clinton* is another example and a perfect illustration of how the makeover narrative affects female politicians in particular. In the book, Buchanan explains how in the beginnings of her political career Hillary started out paying little attention to her hair, "holding it off her face with a headband and leaving its natural color unchanged."[16] However, while US President Barack Obama admitted he was allowed to keep his wardrobe choices to a minimum to avoid decision fatigue, Hillary Clinton's attempt to do the same was met with a lot of criticism. Because she didn't conform to the societal expectation that she pay a lot of attention to her appearance, Hillary was ridiculed, and so "she did what her critics seemed to demand": she got a makeover and had her hair styled and highlighted. After the makeover she was then ridiculed for trying several different hairstyles which became a way of interpretation of her character: "she was too changeable, too concerned with appearances."

It would seem the media's view of women is a reflection of a deeply embedded and socialized double standard that

---

16   Angela Marie Buchanan, *The Extreme Makeover of Hillary (Rodham) Clinton*, (Washington, DC: Regnery Pub, 2007)

evaluates men and women with different standards and different criteria when it comes to judging how they present themselves. It is a double standard that equates masculinity with substance and femininity with artifice. It sees feminine traits as less desirable, but also sees women without feminine traits as less desirable. It is a system of judgment that can overlook the appearance of a man, yet can't see past that of a woman's. It expects women to edit themselves but still punishes them for not being that way naturally, all the while celebrating men who are "unedited." It is a double standard that makes any standard impossible to actually meet. It's a catch-22.

That being said, it is important to note the media isn't necessarily dominated by men with a sexist agenda to which they judge and present all female candidates through a misogynistic lens. The criticism isn't coming solely from men, but from women too. Surprise! Women are capable of being misogynistic and participating in sexist discourse, too! In fact, some of the most callous commentary on Sarah Palin and Hillary Clinton has come from women. With the number of snide comments and backhanded compliments being thrown around by women at female politicians, we could make another sequel to *Mean Girls*. So, for all the #Girlpower and #Feministfightclub trends we have taking place on social media, women have a long way to go, as well in terms of practicing what we preach and actually supporting one another instead of bringing each other down.

CHAPTER 3:

BAD MOM

———

Jacinda Ardern was admitted to Auckland City Hospital on 21 June 2018, and gave birth to a girl at 4:45 p.m., becoming only the second elected head of government to give birth while in office (after Benazir Bhutto in 1990).[17] The announcement of Ardern's pregnancy, accompanied by the news she would be taking baby leave and entrusting her partner Clarke Gayford with the majority of day-to-day parenting, was greeted with a flurry of media attention. Even months before her pregnancy announcement, national and international news outlets weighed in, discussing whether Jacinda was planning on being "in labor or in labor." (referring to whether or not she would be choosing her baby over choosing her party).[18] Although Arden said she was fine with questions being asked about how she was planning on balancing her career with her new child, she added her decision to about it was personal decision and "for other women, it is totally unacceptable in 2017 to say women should have to answer that question in

---

17   Charlotte Graham-McLay, "New Zealand's Leader, Jacinda Ardern, Delivers a Baby Girl" *The New York Times*, June 21, 2018.

18   Camila Domonoske, "New Zealand Political Leader Quizzed On Whether She'll Have Kids" *NPR.org,* August 2, 2017.

the workplace. It is the woman's decision about when they choose to have children. It should not predetermine whether or not they are given a job or have job opportunities." When she finally did give birth, on returning to Parliament after a six-week maternity leave, Ardern expressed the hope her daughter's arrival may pave the way for a change in the way we view mothers in politics. She hoped one day it will be perceived as normal for women to give birth while in office.

High profile women politicians have long confronted a "mommy problem." Political scientist Dr. Jessica Smith from the University of Southampton does research on parenthood, gender, and political leaders; she says despite changing roles in society, the idea or expectation of women's role and value as Mother remains prominent. The "stereotype of women as primary caregivers" is still "very much a lens we like to see women through," she told the BBC. I organized a call to talk with Dr. Jessica Smith about stereotypes in relation to women in politics. She noted that seeing women in positions of political leadership can challenge ingrained cultural assumptions about women's role in society. "We are socialized to value women as mothers," she said, and we are conditioned to want (or at least expect) to see them keeping house and spending time with their children, fulfilling their "biological roles" in the domestic realm. Because of this, when women were finally allowed to enter the political sphere, they ended up bringing an interest in the private and domestic sphere with them. In this way, Dr. Smith argues the trend of increased "personalization" of politics may be gendered as it coincides with women's re-entry into the public sphere. One way women may demonstrate competence in the public sphere is by using the domestic, creating maternal mandate where female elected representatives have to pass the *Good House-keeping* seal of approval: a good mother, a good cook, a great family organizer, and a juggler of competing commitments.

At the same time, however, we also go and pick on women in the workplace for doing exactly that. Women are often berated by male and female bosses alike for not being able to work overtime due to domestic commitments or for having to deal with homelife interruptions. Stories of mothers failing to receive promotions because they had to pick up one too many calls from home or being let go because supervisors said they are tired of having to accommodate mothers with hectic schedules are not unheard of in the workplace, and in fact they are relatively common.

I sat down with my mum to ask her whether she had experienced these things, and I was surprised to hear how many times she had felt like a bad employee for taking phone calls from home or for giving up work time to take care of myself and my brother. There were also times were she felt like a bad mother for saying no every now and then after receiving calls from the school nurse asking her to pick us up from school at 11:00 a.m. because we had a tummy ache (most likely us trying to get out of a homework assignment). She asked me if I had ever considered calling dad in those moments and, shamefully, my answer was no because I felt Mum's work was okay to interrupt but Dad's was off-limits. My mum specifically reflected on the time I managed to wind up in an ambulance on the way to the hospital after eating a blizzard from Dairy Queen (I'm allergic to nuts) while she was at work. She had taken the bus that day and so when the paramedics called her to tell her she needed to come back immediately, she told them she couldn't make it because she was on the other end of town without a car. She said she remembers the paramedics not being very impressed and questioning why she let me (thirteen years old) be home alone in the first place with a nut allergy. While we eventually got a hold of my dad and he was able to come and meet me at the hospital, I remember being upset my mum wasn't "there for me like she was supposed to be as a mother," even though I wouldn't have had a problem if my dad was unable to make it. My mum did not just get in trouble with me, and with the paramedics, but was also told off by her boss at the time for taking that call during work hours. My mum's experience highlights the conventional storyline we have that mothers work less and are more distractible when on the job, and ultimately enforces the idea women can't work and be a mother; you either sacrifice your career for your family or sacrifice your family for your career.

At the risk of stating the obvious, male politicians are not typically asked whether they're sacrificing their dreams of a family for their dream career, and this is likely because, unlike women, they don't have to. Most career paths have been developed with men's lives in mind and have embedded in them the assumption the individual can devote almost all their time to work because someone—usually a non-working wife—is looking after everything else. This double standard is closely tied to misogynistic assumptions about the role and value of women in society and the gendered divide we have in domestic care work—as some might call it, "the mother-hood trap."

The "motherhood trap" ultimately exposes one of capitalism's most uncomfortable secrets—the way it relies on so much unpaid labor, often from women, to sustain itself. Researchers call this the "second shift," which is the idea that when a woman gets home at the end of the day, she must clock into her second, unpaid job—buying groceries, cooking, cleaning and doing dishes, plus "the invisible work" like planning, coordinating, and anticipating the needs of their partner and/or children. When discussing this concept with Dr. Smith, she noted domestic labour comes at the expense of political career opportunities and lifetime earning power for women. While the pay gap between men and women in their twenties is essentially eradicated, a maternity gap still exists, and women's wages never recover from the time devoted to childbearing. Whether it is the fact mothers can't be available to answer emails at all hours or they miss out on the networking that comes with drinks after work, for women who try to combine caring for children with fulfilling their political career aspirations, it often ends up being far too much work to handle. Because of this assumption (and oftentimes the reality) that women will be the ones keeping house and will not be able to handle the double burden of both public and private labour, "party gatekeepers are hesitant to select female candidates, and female candidates are hesitant to run" says Dr. Smith. Ultimately, it seems our current system is set up so "motherhood and politics end up at odds with one another."

So, if female politicians do bear children they are presented with the issue of balancing their work life and domestic responsibilities as a woman, and their capacity to perform as leaders while caring for their families is questioned. Perhaps then it would be easier to just not have children altogether, right?

Unfortunately, it is not that easy.

While women are discriminated against for choosing to have children and are judged for both spending too much time with them and not spending enough time with them, women are also considered suspect for being unable or unwilling to fulfill their presumed biological destiny by choosing not to have children. Sounds like a catch-22 to me.

In 2012 Tony Abbott, the Australian opposition leader, accused the country's prime minister, Julia Gillard, of being "deliberately barren," and implied her non-mother status meant the Australian government was one that "lacks experience in raising children" despite the fact Gillard's cabinet contained members with several children.[19] The comments triggered Julia Gillard's infamous "misogyny speech" in which the prime minister tackled sexism head-on, addressing the rampant misogyny in Australian parliament and condemning the locker-room talk used by Tony Abbott and his peers when talking about women both in and out of their political circles. Despite her riveting speech, however, ABC Radio Senator George Brandis told the show that because Julia Gillard "has chosen not to be a parent…she is very much a one-dimensional person…she just doesn't understand the way parents think about their children when they reach a particular age." Janet Albrechtsen, columnist for *The*

19   Alison Rourke, "Julia Gillard Poll Bounce Following Misogyny Speech"
     The Guardian, March 22, 2012

Australian, wrote, "She has showcased a bare home and an empty kitchen as badges of honor and commitment to her career. She has never had to make room for the frustrating demands and magnificent responsibilities of caring for little babies, picking up sick children from school, raising teenagers. Not to mention the needs of a husband or partner."[20] Additionally, a coalition fundraiser included a satirical menu with a dish described as "Julia Gillard Kentucky Fried Quail— Small Breasts, Huge Thighs & a Big Red Box."[21] Ouch!

Though comments like these tend not to go down very well with the public and the majority of people understand such comments are no longer acceptable, they are still being said. These commenters are saying out loud what many seem to think about childless women: a woman's inexperience as a wife and/or mother makes her and her opinions less valuable in society. In this way, our culture seems to fear the childless woman. Her decision to focus on pursuing personal freedom instead of following her "biological disposition" of raising a family makes her a destabilizing and potentially radical figure. So destabilizing, in fact, that when younger women try to take measures to secure their child-free status, they are sometimes straight-up told no. For example, it took Holly Brockwell, a thirty-year-old woman in Britain, four years to get the National Health Service to tie her fallopian tubes, a simple and somewhat reversible form of sterilization. When Brockwell requested the procedure at age twenty-six, doctors

---

20   Tim Hein, "The 10 Most Publicised Abusive Comments about Julia Gillard," May 21, 2012.

21   Edward Johnson, "Julia Gillard Fried Quail: Small Breasts, Huge Thighs: Australian PM Furious at Opposition Fundraiser Menu" *nationalpost*, June 12, 2013

told her she was "far too young to make such a drastic decision" and she would inevitably change her mind.[22] Of course, few would question a twenty-six-year-old woman's decision to have children, which is arguably just as life-changing of a decision. This situation is not uncommon, and the fact women are vilified as selfish or are seen as incomplete for not having children reveals an uncomfortable truth about how far we still have to go to achieve equality and some redefining of what it really means to be a woman if you're not a mother.

That being said, choosing to pursue a partner and children doesn't make one anti-feminist. I strongly believe women and men should have equal opportunities and choices and receive equal pay for equal work. A woman should be able to have a career and support herself and choose not to marry or to have children, and a man should not considered less masculine if he wants to stay home and care for the kids instead. I also believe, however, both women and men, whether they work or not, should put their children first, and if a woman decides the best way to that is if she stays home, then that is okay too. This was the case with my family; when both my brother and I were born, my mother made the decision to take time out of her career to stay home and look after us. When I asked her whether that was a decision she regretted, and whether she would have preferred to have focused on her career and have my father or someone else look after us, but she said our first years were important to her and she wanted to be there for them at home spending time with us.

22 Holly Brockwell, "I Fought a Four-Year Battle with the NHS to Be Sterilised at 30 - and Won" *Telegraph*, March 24, 2016

Ultimately, the goal is that women can have the freedom to choose, one way or the other, and both choices are something we accept and celebrate. After all, having choices does not imply we should, but that we can if we want to. But just how free that choice actually is when much of society still expects women to choose to be mothers, and frown upon women leaders for both having and not having children, is something worth considering.

CHAPTER 4:

CAN WOMEN REALLY HAVE IT ALL?

———

When it comes to having to make tough decisions between committing to work life and home life, Pamela Hay is an expert. As a Canadian diplomat and current head of the commercial section of the embassy of Canada in Bern, Switzerland, Pamela has lived in four foreign countries on diplomatic postings while raising two daughters (and a few pets) along the way. Through her world travels, Pamela has spent time interacting with women across many different cultures and continents, observing the similarities surrounding the female struggle to find balance and equality at work and at home. This led her to write her book called *Having It All By Not Doing It All: Goodbye Superwoman*, a book reflecting on the struggles women face as mothers and as partners in dealing with the unequal burden of domestic responsibilities at home.[23] I had the opportunity to call Pamela across time

---

23   Pamela Hay, *Having It All by Not Doing It All: Goodbye Superwoman*, (Balboa Press, 2017) Kindle.

zones in Switzerland to chat with her about her book and discuss the challenges career women face in trying to juggle and balance their busy lives.

We began by talking about the importance of raising awareness of gender inequality at home as well as in the workplace. When it comes to our conversations surrounding the progress of gender equality, Pamela said, "the domestic side of things is not talked about enough." The idea behind emancipation was that as women started taking up roles in the workforce and contributing to the bread-winning, men should naturally begin to do more housework and childcare, thereby sharing and reducing the woman's traditional household workload. However, it didn't exactly play out this way. While women have successfully entered the professional world and taken on equal responsibilities to their male counterparts, men haven't necessarily been taking quite so much equal responsibility in the home, leaving most women to take on the burden of working a "second-shift" at home when they get back from work.

For equality to be achieved there needs to be balance. Not only do women need to be given equal opportunity to set foot in the career world, but they also need the opportunity to take a foot out of the domestic one. Without such a balance, women become overloaded with work and end up burning out.

Pamela noted she had experienced this very problem as a professional woman. After years of taking the lead in caring for her children, ex-husband, aging parents, pets, and also saddled with most of the chores at home while working a full-time job, she felt extremely burnt out. When it came to her job and an opportunity for promotion, "I made a conscious decision to stop aiming higher," Pamela said, not because she wasn't "leaning in" but because she genuinely could not handle the burn out from "leaning in" anymore.

In her book she noted that many other women she has met have experienced the same issue. The problem with this trend of second-shifting, overtaxed mothers is that being burnt out is not only harmful for mothers themselves, but also for their children who are watching, listening, and learning from their parent's behaviors and experiences. Pamela references a study done by a journal of the *Association for Psychological Science* that showed that "the best indicator of a girl's ambition is if her father does housework."[24] The study, which involved 326 children aged seven to thirteen and at least one of their parents, looked at the division of chores and paid labour in each household and determined the career stereotypes participants identified with, their gender and work attitudes, and the children's career aspirations. The study found that while mothers' gender and work equality beliefs were key factors in predicting kids' attitudes toward gender, the strongest predictor of daughters' own professional ambitions was their fathers' approach to household chores. More simply, the fact a mother worked outside the home was not as strong a predictor of young girls' aspirations than seeing their father clean the kitchen and fold the laundry. The researchers came to the conclusion that daughters use their mother's experience to gauge whether or not they can manage a career.

---

24 "Dads Who Share the Load Bolster Daughters' Aspirations" Association for Psychological Science, APS, accessed February 1, 2021.

When they see their fathers helping out and pitching in, they are more likely to believe they can find a similar relationship that will allow them to continue to pursue their career aspirations. Meanwhile, one can also assume if sons see an unequal burden of responsibility between their parents at home, and watch their fathers shifting domestic responsibilities onto their mothers, they are more likely to expect as well as enact those same roles when they are older, allowing the cycle to continue.

I am thankful I have a father who has never tried to evade household chores, has taught my brother, as well as myself the importance of pitching in at home, and has supported my mother in pursuing her own career aspirations. My mum is arguably the CEO of our house; she remembered the names of our schoolteachers and friends and the due dates for our projects when my brother and I were younger. She planned our dinners, and assigned our household chores, but my dad would never turn down an opportunity to help out when he was at home and tried his hardest to distribute the responsibilities in our house as evenly as possible. My dad is one of the most hardworking people I know, and he has certainly set a high standard for my partner in the future as well as shown me the most wonderful example of how to be a worker, a partner, and a parent. It is because of this example I feel certain in my desire and ability to pursue the passions, career goals, and leadership positions I aspire to have.

On the topic of equality in the home, Anne-Marie Slaughter's infamous 2013 TED Talk *Can We Really "Have It All"?* also advocates for the balancing of burdens at home, but looks at the idea of domestic equality with a new perspective.[25] Slaughter points out when it comes to talking about inequality in the domestic context, we need to also discuss the ways in which a large part of women hold implicit bias against men and "actually think that they, as women, are naturally more capable than men in the domestic realm," from kids to kitchens. Men, starting from a very young age, are consequentially "aware of a widespread female presumption that we really do know better when it comes to home and kids."

Consider the following scenario: You, a woman, walk into your office on your first day of work and your boss, a man, says, "As a man, I have evolved biologically to do this job better than you can, but I'm going to let you try. However, to be sure it's done right, I will leave you detailed instructions for every individual task, and when I travel, I will call in every couple of hours to make sure you are following those instructions and I will check in to see if you need any help because the work isn't suited to your natural capabilities." You would flip out, wouldn't you? Not only that, but the story would make the news and that boss would probably be fired, and rightly so. So why, then, is this precisely the way many women treat their male partners or family members when leaving them in charge of domestic duties such as cooking, cleaning, or taking care of children?

If a man is told repeatedly that he is not good at cooking, cleaning, or childcare, or that the family is better off if the woman does more of it, he will probably start believing it

---

25   Anne-Marie Slaughter, *Can We All "Have It All"?* Filmed June 2013 at
      TEDxGlobal, Video.

and will likely shy away from participating and/or helping out with those tasks. I believe this is a problem for both men and women equally, as it reinforces the stereotypes that strengthen the barriers which keep men away from the home and pressures them to be breadwinners, and keeps women in the home, unpaid and unable to succeed in the working world and support herself financially. And so, while Anne-Marie emphasizes she is still "completely committed to the cause of male-female equality," she suggests full equality "does not just mean valuing women on male terms...It means creating a much wider range of equally respected choices for women and for men." It also means "valuing family just as much as work and understanding the two reinforce each other." Without this understanding, equality just won't happen, especially in terms of representation of women in politics, because as Pamela Hay noted, "women will just end up being burned out."

The fact we measure male-female equality solely by how many women are able to be in the top leadership positions—prime ministers, presidents, CEOs, directors, managers, Nobel laureates—leaves out a large part of the picture of what true equality looks like. When it comes to female electability, we have to pay attention to more than just equal numbers and equal treatment of women represented at the top. We must also be paying attention to equality in the home. Women aren't going to be able to "have it all" and enjoy their new-found acceptance into the working world if they are working overtime to keep things running at home as well. Unfortunately, no one can do it all. It seems rather silly to think one could in the first place. As an individual, between partners, and within a society, there needs to be balance; we need to acknowledge the importance of both home and work life and support each other in committing to both. Anne-Marie Slaughter put it best when she says "real equality means equality at home just as much as at work."

CHAPTER 5:

SHRILL

———

I grew up in a Christian household. I went to Sunday school as a child and even attended a Christian summer camp, both of which I loved. I also, however, gained a decent knowledge of the Bible, and there was a line in it that always bothered me. In 1 Cor. 14:34 reads, "Women are to be silent in the churches. They are not permitted to speak, but must be in submission, as the Law says."

Obviously times have changed, and this line is, for the most part, not taken literally. Nevertheless, the idea little girls, and women by extension, should be seen and not heard is age-old. In the fourth century BC Aristotle wrote women are "more opinionated, more apt to scold and strike...more false of speech." Shakespeare's 1590 *Taming of the Shrew* champions the story of a husband's success in turning his problematically, opinionated, and headstrong bride into a gentle and submissive one by depriving her of food and sleep. In 1959, when a blonde-haired, blue-eyed pull string talking doll popularized the term "Chatty Cathy," it became a frequently used phrase to refer to a woman who "talks incessantly without saying anything of consequence."

Fast forward to 2017 when Arianna Huffington led a meeting with her staff at Uber to discuss the company's workplace culture, which had been receiving complaints and allegations of sexism and harassment. Arianna spoke to the importance of having gender diversity in the workplace, noting "there is a lot of data that shows when there is one woman on the board, it's much more likely there will be a second woman on the board," but was interrupted by investor and finance veteran David Bonderman who cut in to say, "I'll tell you what it shows is that there's much more likely to be more talking on the board."[26]

What's funny about this stereotype is it's just straight up wrong. Evidence shows women don't actually talk more at all. In fact, when it comes to talking in public settings, it is the other way around; men talk more, interrupt more, and speak for longer than women do. This is evidenced in a review of fifty-six studies that analyze the amount of talk used by American women and men in different contexts. The research, which was conducted by Canadian linguistics researcher Deborah James and social psychologist Janice Drakich, found only two studies showing women talked more than men, while thirty-four studies found men talked more than women.[27] Sixteen of the studies found they talked the same and four showed no clear pattern. The review demonstrated the amount people talk is instead most likely

---

26 Anita Balakrishnan, "Uber Board Member Who Helped Lead Sexism Investigation Joked That Uber's Female Board Members Talk Too Much" *CNBC,* June 13, 2017.

27 James Deborah and Janice Drakich, "Understanding gender differences in amount of talk: A critical review of research" Oxford University Press, (1993).

related to the status of the person given the kind of setting in which the conversation occurs. In public settings, those with higher social status will talk more, while in private settings, status is less important and there is a greater emphasis on taking turns. According to the research, in the public, formal context, men might talk more than women because talking is conceivably aimed at informing or persuading which enhances their status, and men seem to be more concerned with asserting status and power than women are. By contrast, in more private contexts, women might talk more as talk usually serves interpersonal functions and women, it seems, are willing to talk more in relaxed social contexts, especially where the talk functions to develop and maintain social relationships.

So, if men continue to dominate conversation in large social situations, as the studies have shown, why are women still labelled as Chatty Cathy and continuously portrayed by the media as loud, opinionated, and endlessly nagging in co-ed conversations? These stereotypes of women's talk are not only wildly inaccurate, but also come at a significant cost. By treating women's voices as marginal and unwelcome, women are discouraged to compete for and pursue promotions and leadership positions, therefore acting as a very real obstacle to women's contribution to and success in the professional arena. For example, many unapologetically vociferous male politicians and pundits attacked Hillary Clinton for being "shrill," "high-pitched," and "cackling" during her presidential campaign speeches. Donald Trump himself took to Twitter to chastise Clinton's, "very average scream." The tone of her voice, something which Hillary has limited control over, was routinely brandished against her throughout her entire election process. While many reasons can be found as to why Hilary lost to Trump, and it would be a simplification to say the people's distaste for her voice was the only thing that made her unelectable, I do think it played a part. In this way, while the assessment someone "sounds presidential" is typically used to describe the substance of what a candidate is saying, how they say it—the micro-nuances of their speech patterns, and how voters and viewers hear them—can also provide a fascinating window into how we perceive authority and who occupies it.

In a course called Sounding American at the University of California at Berkeley, Tom McEnaney, a professor of comparative literature, teaches his students about the sound people associate with authority in this country and its roots in early broadcast technology.[28] Dating back to the phonograph, he said engineers had created a device designed for the male voice—newscasters, presidents, public figures—to the extent that if a woman spoke into it, her voice would sound thin and distorted. "The mic wouldn't pick up certain ranges of voice," Professor McEnaney said. "If a woman wanted to speak and get her voice recorded, she had to produce more volume and more energy to make the same marks. She could try to speak lower, or she could shout. But she'd have to change her voice." In other words, there was a bias in the engineering. That bias in the engineering produced distortion, which was mistakenly associated with women's voices, and then listeners, even after that correction, used that association as the justification for their ongoing prejudice against women's

28   Jessica Bennett, "What Do We Hear When Women Speak?" *The New York Times*, November 20, 2019.

voices. Over time, that technology improved, but McEnaney thinks the "deep-rooted association between female voices and sonic distortion" is what has led to the overwhelmingly negative reaction many people have to higher pitches and has, furthermore, become the justification for "ongoing prejudice against women's voices," which "carry up to the present day." Besides the fact voice technology was made with men rather than women in mind, women and men tend to have different speech patterns. Women, especially young women, tend to have more versatile intonation. They place more emphasis on certain words; they are playful with language and have shorter and thinner vocal cords, which produce a higher pitch. That isn't absolute, nor is it necessarily a bad thing—unless, of course, you are a person with a higher pitch trying to present yourself with some kind of authority. This basic contradiction has kept speech coaches in business for decades.

Due to the "shrill" claims that dogged Hillary Clinton in both of her campaigns for presidency, Clinton famously paid $7,500 to train with voice and drama coach extraordinaire Michael Sheehan. They worked on deepening her voice in an attempt to give herself more authority during her speech, and with the hopes that by sounding more like a man, maybe she would be treated and judged with the same respect as one. But the 2016 election changed everything. Clinton's choice to train with a voice coach and self-edit her voice and speaking style in her 2016 campaign meant her matchup against Trump left her sounding grimly calculated and inauthentic to critics. Words like "aloof" and "inauthentic" were used simultaneously with "shrill" and "cackling" (confusingly oxymoronic, I know) to describe her personality and her speeches.[29] Clinton herself regrets this. In her memoir *What Happened,* she wrote: "Maybe I have over-learned the lesson of staying calm, biting my tongue, digging my fingernails into a clenched fist. Smiling all the while, determined to present a composed face to the world."[30] By contrast, Trump's "screw the teleprompters" brand of public speaking looked like the real deal to some voters. In this way, the 2016 election sent women a message: playing it safe doesn't always work, and even if you tone it down, you can still get knocked out of the game.

Walking the line between powerful and personal is something we expect leaders to do with ease, but that path is, as evidenced, more difficult to navigate for women. We tell women to talk in a lower pitch, prune their emotion, refrain from laughing, and ultimately sound like a man, but then criticize them for sounding inauthentic when they do. It leaves women, again, in a catch-22 situation. No matter which way they speak, someone finds a problem with it, and on the off chance it works and they manage to get the balance just right enough to pass by criticism, women who deliberately smudge their personalities and tamp down their voices to play it safe often find the resulting fit an uncomfortable one. It's hard to fully exercise your power when you feel compelled to sound like someone you're not and when it comes to women in political leadership positions, it's a wonder they speak up at all.

---

29   Jessica Bennett, "What Do We Hear When Women Speak?" The New York Times, November 20, 2019.

30   Hillary Rodham Clinton, *What Happened,* (New York: Simon & Schuster, 2017)

CHAPTER 6:

LITTLE MISS BOSSY

———

A 2003 Harvard study found that when a man is successful he is liked by both men and women, but when a woman is successful she is *less* liked by both genders.

The study was conducted by researchers who carried out their experiment on students in a Harvard class.[31] The class was split into two groups. Both groups were given an identical case study about a real-life entrepreneur who described how they became a very successful venture capitalist by using their outgoing personality and networking skills. However, for the purposes of the study, one group read about an entrepreneur called Heidi and another group read about an entrepreneur called Howard (the text was identical for both groups, except for the name change). Both groups were then asked a series of questions about the entrepreneur to ascertain how people felt about the entrepreneur's personality. One would think the results would be identical from both groups, but this did not turn out to be the case. The consensus was both were

———

31   Kathleen L. McGinn, and Nicole Tempest, "Heidi Roizen" Harvard Business School Case 800-228, January (2000).

equally competent, but they liked Howard and not Heidi. The student's justification for their judgment was Heidi was seen as selfish and not "the type of person you would want to hire or work for." Here, the man was likeable and the woman was unlikeable, despite being labelled with the same descriptive adjectives. Interesting, right?

The study shows success and likability are positively correlated for men and negatively correlated for women. When a man is successful, he is liked by both men and women, but when a woman is successful, people of both genders like her less. Further research into this phenomenon has shown the existence of two primary kinds of gender bias called descriptive and prescriptive bias, which create this effect for women. Descriptive bias refers to the labels we attach and associate with how certain social groups and communities are, and prescriptive bias refers to how we think these groups and communities should be. Women, for instance, are traditionally described with words like caring, warm, deferential, emotional, and sensitive while men are described as assertive, rational, competent, and objective. When someone does not conform to the stereotypical roles and behaviors prescribed to their gender, they can be penalized or punished. In addition to this, when a woman does not fit the role traditionally assigned to her and attempts to claim a traditionally male position, she is seen as breaking the norm. So, when a woman exhibits traditionally "masculine" qualities such as assertiveness, forcefulness, and ambition, she is labelled as "bitchy," unfeminine, and aggressive, and hence generally disliked. Therefore, for the same kind of leadership behavior, women might be penalized while a man is commended because traits considered "bossy" in women are considered leadership qualities in men. "Bossy" is a word I am somewhat familiar with myself.

When I was four years old, I had a lot of energy. I loved learning, I liked talking to others, and I was described, at least by my parents, as an enthusiastic and strong-willed child with a lot of ambition. When my parents went into my old elementary school to talk to my kindergarten teacher about my progress, however, they received a different story. My mother was told by the teacher I was "quite bossy" and was asked if she herself was bossy, as perhaps it was a "hereditary issue." I had specific ideas about how games should be played and liked to choose which characters everyone got to be or made-up rules about how things should be done. Since most four-year-olds aren't exactly known for their tactfulness, my parents were surprised this was such an issue for my teacher, but apparently I was a little too headstrong and "liked telling people what to do" just a bit too much for her liking. Fittingly, I was then given the *Little Miss Bossy* book from the Little Man series by my family as a joke for Christmas, and so my nickname became "Little Miss Bossy."

While my family and I were able to take the comment as a joke and I continued on with my "enthusiastic" and "strong-willed" ways, the trend of calling little girls bossy is an all-too common one and can be rather problematic when it comes to the issue of female leadership. By calling a little girl "bossy" for being outspoken, we end up teaching girls to back away from leadership roles out of fear of not fitting in. This negative association may lead to the conclusion that if a young girl wants to be liked, she should be quiet and subdued, and keep her thoughts and opinions to herself. If we want to raise strong women, we have to raise strong girls, and that starts with reframing the gendered words we choose to describe them (and all women) with.

Unfortunately, however, this kind of gendered language is particularly visible in the world of political media coverage. A study done by the *Columbia Journal Review* (CJR) wanted to find out whether journalists who write about women running for political office may, consciously or not, choose gender-coded words to describe these candidates and whether these descriptors might in turn affect how the public views these candidates.[32] They asked 269 university students to read a newspaper article from *The Globe and Mail* about a small-town mayoral race. In different versions of the article, the researchers changed the gender of the political candidate and the words used to describe them, but everything else about the articles was exactly the same: one version used feminine-coded descriptive language (words like "compassionate" and "loyal"), one used masculine-coded language ("ambitious," "assertive"), and one used neutral language ("friendly," "adaptable"). Readers were then asked to rate how qualified they thought the candidate was on a ten-point scale and to indicate how much they liked the candidate on a 101-point scale. Such language choices, the study found, do have an impact. A woman politician described with masculine-coded adjectives was seen as almost 10 percent more qualified and 7 percent more competent than a woman described with feminine adjectives. These effects might seem small, but they are substantively large and might have serious implications for

---

32 Rachel Garrett and Dominik Specula, "Subtle Sexism in Political Coverage Can Have a Real Impact on Candidates" Columbia Journalism Review (2018).

elections, especially at the local level where people are less reliant on party cues and more reliant on their perception of candidates' traits. Since people today rely almost exclusively on the media as their source of political information, the type of coverage and choice of words used to describe politicians in media coverage has a huge influence on voters' perceptions.

In the lead up to the 2020 election, a large portion of voters in the USA told reporters they would consider voting for a woman. Nevertheless, the 2020 election's democratic primary, which began with six diverse women candidates, essentially came down to two white men: former Vice President (and eventual winner) Joseph R. Biden Jr. and Senator Bernie Sanders, not because the public didn't like the women candidates, but because they felt Biden, as a white man, had the best shot at defeating President Trump. This is because voters strategically change who they vote for to match what they believe the rest of the electorate thinks. If a voter believes a large portion of the electorate is not ready for a woman president, they may choose to vote for a male candidate who they believe has a greater chance of winning. This calculus is often justified by beliefs about other people's sexism—an Ipsos/*Daily Beast* poll in June, for example, found only 33 percent of Democrats and Independents said they believed their neighbors would be comfortable with a female president. While they themselves didn't mind the idea of a woman president, the things they saw and heard in the news and on social media gave them the impression the rest of America just wasn't ready for one yet.[33] In this way, we can see how

---

33   Chris Jackson, "Nominating Woman or Minority Come Second to Nominating Candidate Who Can Beat Trump" *Ipsos* (2020).

disadvantageous reporting of female politicians in the media, even in subtle forms, is enough to push people away from supporting women candidates.

The sum of all these things means gender bias in reporting by the media can depress the political ambitions of young women and discourage the public from supporting, and selecting women to be in leadership roles, ultimately leading to continued underrepresentation of women in the future. Simply put, words matter. Call a little girl "bossy" and she starts to avoid leadership roles because she's afraid of being seen as unlikeable. Call a woman "aggressive" out loud and her boss will probably pass her over for a promotion. Call a female politician a "ballbuster" enough times and people may actually be less likely to vote for her.

Words can have a powerful impact on perception, and perception has a powerful impact on how we think and act. This is especially the case when it comes to gender bias against female leaders.

CHAPTER 7:

HYSTERICAL

———

According to a study done by Georgetown University Center on Education and the Workforce (CEW), 13 percent of Americans (roughly one in ten), still believe men are better "emotionally suited" for politics than women.[34] This figure surprises me, especially considering the fact previous president Donald Trump, a man, displayed the emotional control of four-year-old during his time in office. The CEW study notes while this figure is lower than it's ever been—in 1975 nearly 50 percent of Americans held this belief—it is still big enough to "cause candidates to lose elections." Despite the undeniable progress, female candidates continue to face a significant bias against them that has absolutely nothing to do with their abilities or qualifications. That bias, the Georgetown report notes, "weeds out potential candidates on the basis of stereotypes" and "arguably prevents voters from electing the most capable and qualified leaders."

———

34   Kristen Bellstrom, "13% of Americans Think Women Are Less 'Emotionally Suited' to Politics Than Men" *Fortune,* April 16, 2019.

The notion of women being emotionally intemperate is age-old. In both Ancient Egypt and Ancient Greece, philosophers and early physicians believed any physical or mental trouble in a woman was caused by a "wandering womb" which interfered with other bodily and brain functions in the process.[35] The idea a woman's psyche was controlled by her reproductive organs continued on into the seventeenth century, in part fueling the spread of "hysteria" during the Salem Witch Trials in Massachusetts in 1692. It wasn't until 1980 hysteria was finally disbanded as an official psychiatric disease. However, while the term is officially out of the medical lexicon, it has managed to stick around and stick particularly to women. The infamous 2016 presidential debate in which Trump referred to Fox News host Megan Kelly as hysterical is an example, with Trump telling CNN's Don Lemon, "You could see there was blood coming out of her eyes...blood coming out of her wherever."[36] Trump's comments came after Megan Kelly pressed Trump about the misogynistic, sexist comments he made in referring to women as "fat pigs, dogs, slobs, and disgusting animals." Here, the ancient practice of women being seen as hysterical for disagreeing with their male-counterparts came back into play.

Megan Kelly is not alone in being referred to as hysterical and "off base." Julia Gillard, former prime minister of Australia known for her speech in 2012 Australian Parliament where she called out the sexist attacks that were directed at her

---

35   Lindsey Fitzharris, "The Wandering Womb: Female Hysteria through the Ages" *Dr Lindsey Fitzharris* (blog), April 28, 2017, accessed January 3, 2021.

36   Holly Yan, "Trump Draws Outrage after Megyn Kelly Remarks" *CNN Politics*, August 8, 2015.

by the oppositional party, was also called "hysterical" and "brittle." Interestingly, the opposition party also picked up the choice phrase of "ditch the witch" to attack Gillard. It seems as though we could teleport back to 1692 Massachusetts and still fight right in. Isn't that worrying? Six years after her speech, Gillard has become one of the icons of the gender movement. In an interview with Blair Williams about her struggles during her prime ministership, Gillard spoke to the impossible and very contradictory standards she felt she had to hold herself to when it came to portraying any emotion.[37] "You hold yourself back from getting too angry, too animated, too passionate because you're fearful of being labelled as hysterical or shrill," Ms. Gillard said in the interview. At the same time, however, you also have to "hold yourself back from being too emotional…because you're too worried about being criticized as soft. You end up walking quite a narrow behavioral pathway…I think it's no mystery women leaders are often therefore described as 'aloof,' 'robotic,' and 'cold.'"

Julia Gillard makes a very good point. To be considered charismatic, leaders must be both appealing and inspiring, both likable and visionary. Unfortunately, women who seek positions of power are rarely perceived as possessing these characteristics at the same time as being deemed competent to do the job. To academics who study women leaders, this wouldn't come as a surprise. Catalyst, a research group focusing on women's experience in the workplace, has noted that, compared to men, "women spend additional time during

---

37 Blair Williams, "From Tightrope to Gendered Trope: A Comparative Study of the Print Mediation of Women Prime Ministers" PhD Thesis, College of Arts & Social Sciences, The Australian National University (2020).

work hours proving they are competent leaders."[38] The reason, according to continued research done in a 2010 study by Victoria Brescoll and Erica Dawson of Yale University and Eric Luis Uhlmann of INSEAD, is that women in traditionally male jobs "are penalized more harshly for making mistakes. Their status and competence [are] fragile and more easily revoked."[39] The problem is in taking extra precautions to avoid mistakes, they came across as less visionary. Because women leaders "often lack the presumption of competence accorded to their male peers," they "are less likely to go out on a limb, extrapolating from facts and figures to interpretations that are more easily challenged...They adopt a defensive, often rigid posture, relying less on their imagination and creativity." Fearful of coming across as incompetent, women carefully edit themselves, but then often end up appearing as uninspiring as a result. Therefore, in seeking to bolster their fragile reputation for competence, women become less likable, and then they become unelectable. Despite this, female leaders are still expected to check every box and exhibit every leadership trait, while men can get away with checking just a few.

My belief is charisma isn't just a personality trait, but a particular relationship between a leader and their followers. I think the emergence of charismatic leaders depends not only on their ability to be their full selves, but also on the public's ability to see their leadership as valid. It is founded

---

38 "The Double-Bind Dilemma for Women In Leadership: Damned If You Do, Doomed If You Don't" Catalyst, accessed December 2020.

39 Victoria L Brescoll, Erica Dawson, and Eric Luis Uhlmann, "Hard Won and Easily Lost The Fragile Status of Leaders in Gender-Stereotype-Incongruent Occupations" Psychological Science 21, no. 11 (2010): 1640-1642.

on the perception and recognition of authority—something which followers give and can just as easily take away—and unfortunately for female candidates, theirs is an authority the public seems to be less willing to recognize. This was evidently the case for Hillary Clinton who was, in the words of Barack Obama, the "most qualified candidate" to ever to seek the presidency, but, according to *The Guardian*, lost the 2016 election because she lacked "authenticity and the kind of charisma required to unite a nation." Elizabeth May, too, has been nicknamed "the Maybot" and been described as "a charisma-free populist" before being booted out of her leadership position.[40] But whether you like Hillary Clinton or Teresa May or not (and there are of course valid reasons not to), even if these women don't seem "likeable," I have a hard time believing any one of these women is more inherently flawed or less likeable than their male counterparts who have been running the country.

---

40   Elizabeth Winkler, "Hillary Clinton's Charisma Deficit Is a Common Problem for Female Leaders" *Quartz*, September 11, 2016.

CHAPTER 8:

ONLY WOMAN AT THE TABLE

———

Do this with me:

Close your eyes. Think of a successful doctor, CEO, politician, president, or prime minister. What do they look like? The images that came to your head were probably ones of old, white men, right?

This is not to say anything is wrong with old white men. Most of us have many of them in our lives and love them dearly, but when people can only picture that image of a white, old man as their leader, without even realizing it we end up pushing away the idea of alternatives (women, people of color, people of different sexualities, etc.) because they just aren't what we are used to or were expecting. Instead, we end up going with the more comfortable choice, with what we have always gone with before, and unfortunately women are neither of those things. The fact that we associate old, white men with leadership means we associate leadership with old, white men, and these preconditioned thoughts and attitudes about what a leader traditionally looks like inevitably plays to the male advantage at the expense of women. Our society thus becomes rigged by an underlying, subconscious bias creating a self-perpetuating cycle of bias against women it comes to choosing, treating, and judging our leaders. Simply put, how is a woman supposed to become a leader if no one gives her the opportunity to show she can be one in the first place? It's hard to be what you (and everyone else) can't see.

Humans tend to be opposed to changes in the status quo until they are forced, through experience, to see that change isn't such a big deal. Yes, we're all probably conditioned in some way to expect men to be leaders and women to be, well, not leaders, but if we interact with an inspiring female boss, we may see the stereotypes for what they are and change our minds. This is where the logic of gender quotas come in. For our society to finally start seeing women leaders as an option, we need to put them there as an option in the first place. In other words, by reserving spots for women, we are levelling the playing field by counteracting the inherent biases we have that work against women. An electoral gender quota for example, which requires at least 40 percent of the candidates on the electoral lists are women, might boost women into leadership positions they would have otherwise been passed over for, and provide them with the opportunity to be seen by others and to show they can be just as competent, capable, and as valuable as their male counterparts. In an ideal world, we wouldn't need to have quotas because we wouldn't have a system of stereotypes or bias or double standards working against women, but until those biases are gone we need a way to combat the barriers that act against women.

That being said, while I want women to be given a boost up to combat these barriers, gender quotas aren't perfect and aren't going to fix gendered leadership inequality in the workplace by themselves. When it comes to leadership, equal opportunity is important, and while quotas can help minimize the impact of barriers that prevent women from their fair share of the political seats, the fact gender quotas give preference to women over men can create problems. For example, I would hate to see an opportunity my father, brother, or partner merited taken away from them just because they are men. I would also hate for a narrative to take hold that female politicians are only elected because of their gender. In addition to that, organizations may hire women in a tokenistic way just to meet quotas and seem diverse but fail to actually create a culture of gender equality in the workplace environment. Providing women with a spot to fulfill the diversity criteria without actually working to change their company's culture, process, and output in a way that equally represents and values women does nothing to actually support women in leadership. In fact, it often ends up creating an "only woman at the table" situation.

About 1 in 5 women say they often end up being the only woman at the table in their workplace, and this experience is about twice as likely for senior-level women and women in technical roles.[41] The expectation seems to be that women should be happy to be slotted here and there into cultures and structures that had been designed entirely by and for men, leaving women to fend for themselves in the workplace.

---

41   "Women in the Workplace," McKinsey, accessed February 11, 2021.

If only one woman is at the table, they become a representative of their entire gender. This primes gendered stereotypes about femininity and the characteristics and capabilities of women in general. When a person is the only woman at the table, their performance is marked with gendered notation, and their successes and failures become a test for what women as an entire gender are capable of. This raises the stakes on any kind of performance, increasing the pressure on women to perform perfectly, without mistakes, so as not to shoot their entire gender in the foot.

Another issue that comes with being an "only" in a male-dominated workplace is that it sets women up to compete against each other, each fighting for one tokenistic spot. I certainly found this to be the case when I entered university classrooms and spaces for the first time. My high school was made up of only girls, so all the "spots at the table" went to girls, meaning competition for leadership positions had nothing to do with gender. At university, however, I noticed an intense air of competition between female students when there were men around. There was a want and a need to impress and to be seen as better than the other women in the room—an interesting observation considering the fact women did not seem to be comparing themselves and be competing with the men. It seems as though when women are all vying for one tokenistic spot, the scarcity creates a female rivalry. In other words, women feel they can't afford to boost each other up for fear of losing their own spot to the competition. If women are too busy fighting amongst themselves for that one spot at the table, we won't be able to band together and fight against the real problem: the fact that there is only one space for women at the table in the first place.

If we want to see a future with strong women leaders, then we need to make sure more than just one sport for women exists at the table. Luckily, some brilliant people out there are working to do exactly that.

PART 2:

CHANGING TIMES FOR FEMALE LEADERS

INTRODUCTION

———

In 2021, we are at a place woman couldn't have even dreamed about just a few years ago. As people are starting to observe more women competently serving as leaders, the idea of a woman being in charge is starting to become less strange. Despite everything mentioned in the first section, times are changing, and they are certainly changing for the better. Although barriers to gender equality in politics are still very much present, women are rising into leadership roles in many nations. With the landmark election of Kamala Harris as vice president, Harris will have risen higher in national leadership than any woman in US history. Harris has become the first woman, Black person, and Indian American to serve as vice president of the United States, and in her own words, she "will not be the last."[42] Furthermore, tales of strong female leaders succeeding through the COVID-19 pandemic bring some hope the overarching narrative of what a strong leader looks like is finally starting to include women. The praise of women leaders in Denmark, Finland, Germany, Iceland,

---

42 Lauren Gambino, "'I Won't Be the Last': Kamala Harris, First Woman Elected US Vice-President, Accepts Place in History" *The Guardian*, November 8, 2020.

Norway, Taiwan, and New Zealand, which will be explored in the coming chapters, point to the possibility of a new wave of female, political role models for the next generations to come and encourage more women positions of political leadership in the future.

Many of these changes are taking place because of the greater willingness of society to have a more open, honest, and vulnerable conversation about the struggles of women in political leadership positions. We are starting to see society actively try and change the way we think about and treat women in politics through the hard work of people, organizations, apps, and industries that are putting effort into promoting gender equality and female leadership. This section explores these changes and looks at how they play a role in supporting women in politics by creating environments inclusive and encouraging of female leaders. The upcoming chapters in this second section of the book will take a look at a variety of people, apps, and organizations pushing back against gender stereotypes and prejudices to help create a more inclusive space for a future of female leaders.

I hope this part can convince you a brighter future is out there for women in leadership, and that as long as we continue to address and work on changing our beliefs and attitudes about gender and leadership, we will be able to overcome the barriers still hindering female leaders. The fact women are finally starting to be seen as important and capable leaders is a great sign of progress, and I believe it points toward a new age of inclusivity for female leaders. I have great hope the women and girls of the future will be able to look at the world around them and see women are indeed electable.

CHAPTER 1:

PANDEMIC POWER PLAYERS

___

The COVID-19 pandemic has taken the world as we know it and flipped it upside down. In the midst of the pandemic, I was in Edinburgh, Scotland, on a student exchange. As the novel coronavirus started traveling across Europe, countries started locking down, closing borders, imposing travel restrictions, and telling people to wear masks and stay home. The UK, however, was a little slow to join the party, and so when the arrival of the novel coronavirus finally reached us, you could say we were in a bit of trouble.

Critics around the world accused the "complacent" British government of "massively underestimating" the gravity of the coronavirus crisis after the UK reported the highest death toll in Europe, with many pointing toward British Prime Minister Boris Johnson's breezy attitude and contradictory declarations as the catalyst.[43] Johnson's government delayed lockdowns and hesitated in following the advice given by experts on implementing crucial protective measures, like increasing testing capacity and ordering safety equipment for hospitals. While Boris Johnson rose to power as a prominent Brexit backer, promising to play hardball to win the best "deal" in the country's exit from the European Union, the strongman skills he used with Brexit didn't turn out to be very useful in the fight against the pandemic. "What we learned with COVID," says Dr. Evans, a sociologist at King's College London studying how women gain power in public life, "is that the traditional idea of the 'strongman leader' who projects power, acts aggressively, and above all shows no fear, might not be as valuable in today's new political era."[44] "Perhaps," he goes on to say, "people will learn to recognize and value risk averse, caring and thoughtful leaders," leaders like Jacinda Arden, whose "approach to fighting the pandemic could not be further from the traditional strongman archetype," but has proved to be successful through her cautious and collaborative strategy. Arden's open, honest, and inclusive leadership is receiving attention around the world, with the public unanimously considering her an "outstanding leader."

However, Jacinda Arden is not the only leader who has been praised for their handling of the pandemic. Germany, led by Angela Merkel, has had a far lower death rate than Britain, France, Italy, or Spain, and Finland, where

---

43   Jon Henley, "'Complacent' UK Draws Global Criticism for Covid-19 Response" *The Guardian*, May 6, 2020.

44   Amanda Taub, "Why Are Women-Led Nations Doing Better With Covid-19?" *The New York Times*, May 16, 2020

thirty-four-year-old Prime Minister Sanna Marin governs with a coalition of four female-led parties, has had fewer than 10 percent as many deaths as nearby Sweden. Tsai Ing-wen, the president of Taiwan, has presided over one of the most successful efforts in the world at containing the virus, using testing, contact tracing, and isolation measures to control infections, without having to implement a full national lockdown. Notice something in common about all these leaders? That's right. They are all women.

In looking at Our World in Data's statistics on COVID-19 deaths by country, I found countries most affected by the COVID-19 pandemic, with an average number of deaths per million of 444.75, are the US, Brazil, Russia, Spain, United Kingdom, Italy, and France, all countries led by male leaders.[45] Meanwhile, the countries led by female leaders such as Germany, Taiwan, New Zealand, Iceland, Finland, Norway, and Denmark have an average number of deaths of only 50.75 per million. It seems then all the praise the female leaders have received is well earned. I mean, you can't argue with the data.

The statistics and stories of the aforementioned success of female leaders in fighting the coronavirus has led some to conclude women just outright make better leaders than men. However, there are many possible reasons as to why this is the case.

45 "Daily vs. Total Confirmed COVID-19 Deaths per Million" Our World in Data, accessed February 11, 2021.

For example, what if countries led by women are managing the pandemic more effectively, not because women are better, but because countries that allow women to be leaders are the ones made up of leaders selected from a larger pool of talent? After all, you don't have to be a math whiz to see if a country rejects 50 percent of its talent for leadership roles, it ends up with less talent. The presence of a female leader, therefore, signals people of diverse backgrounds—and thus, hopefully, diverse perspectives on how to combat crises—are able to win seats at the table when it comes to making important political decisions like those surrounding the coronavirus. Greater involvement of women results in a more holistic perspective on the crisis and paves the way for the deployment of richer and more complete solutions than if they had been imagined by a homogeneous group. An example of this would be Jacinda Arden's Labor Party in New Zealand, which won a landslide victory in the 2020 national election and is projected to form New Zealand's first single-party government in more than two decades. The party had just elected its most diverse parliament ever with 48 percent representation of women as well as sixteen Māori MPs and twelve seats for the LGBTQIA+ community, before tackling the COVID-19 pandemic, and it clearly did so with success.[46] New Zealand was the first country to announce they were COVID-19 free and has incredibly low COVID-19 cases and related deaths in comparison to other countries (and islands) their size. Here, the diversity of parliament and the handling of the pandemic seem to be positively correlated. Coincidence? I personally don't think so, but whichever way you see it, the success of

46 Julia Hollingsworth, "New Zealand Has Just Elected One of the Most Diverse Parliaments in the World. Here's How It Stacks up" *CNN,* November 16, 2020.

female-led countries in handling the pandemic is certainly reshaping notions of female leadership.

The influx of news commentary and conversations about the success of these women-led countries against the COVID-19 pandemic seems to point toward a reckoning with our ideas of what a political leader can look like. The group of female leaders just mentioned may become the new wave of role models for the next generations to come, and the fact that they identify as female may help shift the way we think and redefine the way we evaluate women in the running to be our political leaders in the future. By seeing female leaders succeeding through crisis, we can change the ideas of what a strong leader looks like. For years, there has been an expectation that leaders should be aggressive and forward and domineering (which has made it very difficult for women to thrive as leaders as demonstrating those strongman traits leaves them to be criticized as unfeminine). Stories of female leaders succeeding, displaying both feminine and masculine traits, provides the opportunity to inspire young girls and women who are passionate about politics to step up, participate, and show the world their leadership skills as well. Society at large can therefore foreseeably be less surprised and more comfortable and accepting of female leaders and the unique traits they bring to the table in terms of leadership style.

In the midst of the pandemic, change was also facilitated by the United States 2020 presidential election. Joe Biden's 2020 announcement that California senator Kamala Harris would be named as the Democrats' 2020 candidate for vice president brought us one step closer to answering the question of what it would look like to have a woman sit in office in the

White House as president. As Ms. Harris joins the extremely short list of women who've been nominated for vice president, and with the 2021 inauguration the closest a woman has yet come to office, she will be faced with navigating the complexities of race and gender in her historic nomination.

Ms. Harris is certainly another key woman power player we have seen come to light during the pandemic. Being the first Black woman and the first person of Indian descent to be nominated for national office by a major party, and only the fourth woman in US history to be chosen for a presidential ticket, Harris is paving the way for other women of color to see themselves as potential leaders of the future. This is an ever-important feat considering the current pandemic; we need as many as strong leaders as possible during times of crisis like this. In her DNC nomination speech, Kamala thanked Biden for the nomination, saying herself that "by choosing a woman to run for our nation's second-highest office, you sent a powerful signal to all Americans. There are no doors we cannot unlock."[47] All across the nation, "little girls woke up, especially little Black and brown girls, who so often feel overlooked and undervalued in their communities, but today—today, just maybe, they're seeing themselves for the first time in a new way. As the stuff of presidents and vice presidents," the Democratic nominee said. Senator Harris is a model for little girls; her success sends a message to girls that this is becoming a different world, and possibilities now exist that maybe didn't exist for their mothers or grandmothers.

---

47   Christina Wilkie, "Here's What Kamala Harris Said at the Democratic National Convention" *CNBC*, August 19, 2020.

The impressive political rise of women like Jacinda Arden, Angela Merkel, Tsai Ing-wen, and Kamala Harris is well overdue, and their hard work in breaking the barriers of gender (and race) means other girls and women feel they can find success, too.

CHAPTER 2:

ORGANIZATIONS MAKING CHANGE

———

In the midst of my research about the crisis of female unelectability, I came across the organization She Should Run.[48] As an initiative created by the Commonwealth Women Parliamentarians Canadian Region, She Should Run provides women who are curious about public office with a starting place to explore their own leadership options. The organization's mission is to "increase the pipeline of women considering a run" and works to motivate and encourage women from all political leanings, ethnicities, sexual identities, and backgrounds to see themselves as future candidates and explore the possibility of public office. She Should Run does this by "identifying and tackling the barriers to elected leadership" by providing the tools and resources women leaders need to run. This includes connecting women with a supportive community and providing them with the information they

---

48   "What We Do at She Should Run" She Should Run, accessed January 3, 2021.

need in the form of data-driven content, education, and collective action.

She Should Run facilitates a number of programs that guide women toward discovering different pathways to leadership. One of these programs, The Incubator, provides women with a set of online courses to help users start their path to public service. The Incubator's courses provide thoughtful guidance on how to build upon qualifications, networks, personal story, and leadership brand through the lens of public service. The program also connects women with each other as peer-to-peer mentors as a way of helping women feel comfortable and supported as they explore a run for office. Their Professional Development Series is another program that allows businesses and organizations to develop and retain women leaders by providing teams with actionable strategies to take steps toward pursuing personal leadership and solving gender inequality. This program ultimately encourages organizations to build a healthier, more inclusive workplace for women, and make a time and financial investment in women's leadership and advancement. The philosophy of She Should Run is "when more women run, more women lead." As more and more women become elected officials at all levels of office, through the help of the She Should Run community, they become role models that inspire young girls and young women to do the same. Through their programs, She Should Run ultimately helps women overcome the gendered barriers to politics and be part of creating a more effective and representative government that can meet the challenges of the twenty-first century.

As She Should Run illustrates, representation is a key ingredient to the success of gender equality in politics. Another key ingredient, however, is making sure women's voices are actually heard and valued once they break through that barrier of representation. This is where organizations like Susan Room's organization come in.

Susan Room, a professional voice and executive coach based in the United Kingdom, provides professional coaching to help women find their voice. I was lucky enough to receive the opportunity to organize a call to talk with her and learn more about the way in which voice coaching can be used to help women gain confidence in themselves and overcome gender inequalities and barriers to leadership in the political sphere.

As a former corporate leader and a graduate of the Royal Central School of Speech and Drama, Susan is one of very few coaches qualified to provide both voice and executive coaching. This experience ultimately gives her the expertise to help cultivate a speaking style in women leaders that helps them "use their voice to make their mark on the world." As a former business leader and passionate gender equality advocate, Susan explained her experience as a female business leader in the corporate world played a large part in galvanizing her passion for helping women find their voice. Having been the only female voice in the boardroom for many years, Susan understands how challenging it can be for women to speak up and be heard. As Susan identifies on her website, a long and sexist history of bias is prevalent against the female voice; male voices are typically preferred over female voices, and so men's expression ends up being encouraged while women's expression is discouraged.[49] Because men's voices are valued over women's voices, women therefore tend to lack confidence in their voice and will speak up less. The challenge women face in being heard plays a huge role in preventing women from reaching for and assuming senior leadership roles. This is especially the case in politics which is still a massively male-dominated and male-biased sphere. As Susan notes, women often experience issues of inequality to a greater degree than men and are more directly concerned by certain policy decisions. Because of this, women politicians are more likely to speak with emotion. Unfortunately, this emotion can be perceived as incompetence and can hinder women's professional voice and political goals. As a result, Susan explains, women—especially those who are politicians—"can learn to make strategic vocal choices." To help women with this feat, Susan offers both executive coaching for women and voice coaching for women and has created a program called Make Your Mark with Susan Room where she runs coaching events for women-only groups.

Within her programs and coaching events, Susan works with women to work with their vocal, verbal, and non-verbal communication skills to help them use their voices to express themselves to their full capability. In her own words, Susan helps women "work with what they were born with" and find the full potential of their voices so they can "play it like a musical instrument." The women she has coached have been made partners or have been promoted at work and have found the courage to do more presentations or look for more

---

49   "Susan Room Voice and Executive Coach" Susan Room, accessed January 3, 2021.

opportunities to speak and network. "I firmly believe better balance makes for better business, and I want to see more women in senior roles," Susan explains on her website, "and one way of closing the gap is to coach girls and young women to use their voice and non-verbal communication skills more confidently and effectively." As a result, Susan explains, the work she does in her programs is ultimately about confidence. "If women are more confident in their own voice, they will be more likely to use it, and speak up in the workplace," she says. Susan Room and her voice coaching programs are, in the most basic sense, about helping women to feel, look, and sound more confident so they may come one step closer to achieving the confidence they need to reach their leadership goals and aspirations.

Another organization that helps women reach their leadership goals and aspirations is one that is close to home—McGill Women in Leadership. McGill Women in Leadership is a student-run organization at my university that is dedicated to providing students with the information and a support network necessary to tap into their full potential. The club works to "inspire students by welcoming women from a variety of career fields to share their stories and accomplishments, connect members with extensive opportunities to learn; and ultimately empower them to be critically engaged global leaders." As a club, we host a variety of events throughout the year, such as speaker series', conferences, leadership panels, and other fun awareness-raising and fundraising events. These events ultimately allow McGill Women in Leadership to champion female and feminist empowerment and feminism and provide students with the ability to develop essential skills, gain confidence, and prepare themselves to be strong leaders. This year I have been given the privilege of being able to work with the McGill Women in Leadership club as a director of our outreach portfolio. In our portfolio, my other team members and I strive to develop meaningful relationships with local charities and organizations that support women in our greater Montreal community.

Being part of the McGill Women in Leadership outreach team has helped me see myself as a strong woman leader and has also helped me feel like I am making a difference in my community. Furthermore, through my position I have been able to meet and connect with so many other like-minded students who care about supporting and encouraging fellow women to pursue leadership opportunities. I believe being part of a dynamic group of people who celebrate the leadership and successes of women has encouraged me to be my best, and I am certain this is the case for the other women, too. By bringing women together to collaborate in the development of their leadership skills, McGill Women in Leadership ultimately creates positive change in the future of women's leadership. Ultimately these organizations work to build women's confidence in themselves, and encourage, as well as normalize, women's leadership.

By providing the tools and resources needed to engage, inspire, and empower women, She Should Run, Susan Room, and McGill Women in Leadership help to dismantle the barriers to female leadership and create a brighter future for female politicians. Thanks to organizations like this, women can now see opportunities to electability where they used to see barriers.

CHAPTER 3:

APPS MAKING CHANGE

———

I remember watching the first presidential debate back in September 2016. It was nauseating. Hillary Clinton was interrupted by Donald Trump more than fifty times. As the debate wrapped up and came to an end, I remember thinking to myself: How come even the most powerful women are subject to being spoken over by men? How can people sit back and still think women are valued and treated as equals, especially in politics? Apparently, I wasn't the only one who thought this.

Gal Barradas, who presented *The Right to Finish Talking* at TEDxSanPaolo, was also taken back by the obvious sexism taking place in the election and decided she was going to do something about it.[50] As an avid supporter and participant in executive leader groups for gender equality and in technology-based start-ups, Gal gathered up a team and developed Woman Interrupted, a non-profit app dedicated

---

50 Gal Barradas, *The Right to Finish Speaking,* Filmed September 2017 at TEDxSaoPauloSalon, Video.

to detecting and exposing "manterruption" in everyday interactions.[51] Gal wanted to show the world "Manterruption is real." Woman Interrupted defines manterruption as a sexist behavior that happens precisely when a woman cannot finish her speech because a man unnecessarily interrupts her. The app works by using the microphone on cellular devices to record and analyze the different voices participating in a conversation and uses frequency measurements to determine which voices are male and which are female. It should be noted none of the actual conversations are recorded and stored; everything the microphone picks up goes straight from voice to data to ensure the privacy of the users of the app. After capturing the voice frequency measurements in the conversation, the app can then track the frequency of voices and voice calibrations to identify every instance in which a man interrupts a woman. Every time a male speaker interrupts or speaks over the female speaker, the manterruption is noted in the audio file. Once the user finishes recording the conversation, the audio file is converted into graph form with the amount of "manterruptions" tallied up and presented as a numerical total. The user can then see how many times they were interrupted by men in that conversation, as well as save the data or share it on social media as the app suggests, to start a conversation with others and spread awareness about the issue of manterruption. From this data, Woman Interrupted has also launched a Global Dashboard that presents an overview of the data collected around the world in real time to allow users to find information such as

51   "Woman Interrupted" WomanInterruptedapp, accessed November 3, 2021.

the number of interruptions per minute and per country, as well as comparisons between countries.

I had the opportunity to call Gal and chat with her about her app and the work it does in creating a more inclusive environment for women around the world. Gal explained the app has had huge success since its launch in 2017; it has been downloaded in 154 countries and used in 145 of them. The app has been shown on ABC News with one of the presenters, Emily Evans, using the tool to show her male colleagues just how often she is interrupted on live TV (seventeen times during their live segment) and has been shown in Times Square, receiving an entire panel to advertise the app for a month for free. Gal believes this success is down to the fact women still feel unheard and undervalued in the workplace and are in need of tools to support them in getting their voices heard. "We have worked hard to get women into the workplace, but what does that matter if their voices aren't being heard?" says Gal. For her, it is this lack of female voices in politics that leads to female interests and perspectives receiving less thought, and less priority, and are therefore underrepresented in the policy decisions that are made." We need women present so women's perspectives and needs are actually represented in the policies and decisions that are developed and approved," she says. "Equal voices, as well as equal representation, are an important step in the battle for woman empowerment and gender equality."

Another trailblazer for gender equality in the world of smartphone applications is Amy Cross. As a journalist, an entrepreneur, and the award winner of the 2015 Foreign Policy Global Thinker Award for her work on Economic Girl Power,

Cross is a "longtime cultural worker with a powerful ability to see the next big trend." I was lucky enough to talk to Cross about her game-changing app Gender Fair, which she founded in 2016. The app works by showcasing companies that serve women well and promote gender equality through market-based solutions. Gender Fair rates everyday brands and the companies behind them so shoppers can scan labels or look up products as they shop to make purchasing decisions that support gender equality.[52] By measuring thirteen different data points based on the UN Women Empowerment Principles, the app will tell you how your favorite brands measure up and can then suggest Gender Fair alternatives for those that don't meet the standards. The chosen company or brand has to excel in four major areas—leadership, employee policies, advertising, and philanthropy—to get the stamp of approval. This means performing well when it comes to work/life integration policies such as flex work, telecommuting and employee benefits, producing advertising material which should break any gender stereotypes and norms, and investing and contributing to philanthropic initiatives that support women and girls. Through this, the app ultimately shows companies that consumers care about gender equality and that investing in gender inclusivity and diversity in their workplaces pays off. "Measuring and collecting data on gender equality helps create change," Amy says. "No one wants to do badly on an equity and diversity index," and the existence of this app as a measurement tool ultimately pushes companies to change workplace attitude and environment in a way that better supports women.

---

52 "Our Mission, Gender Fair" GenderFair, accessed December 3, 2021.

When I asked Amy about the inspiration behind her idea, she explained her interest began with politics. Cross notes she "comes from long line of feminists"; her great grandmother was a suffragist and friend of American women's suffragist Frances Willer, and her grandmother was the woman who encouraged her to attend Wellesley College for women (the same university Hillary Clinton attended). As a child, Amy marched with her family for the Equal Rights Amendment in Washington, which sixty years later has still not been ratified. In our conversation, Amy reflected on how disappointing it is to see this is the case. It was because of this feeling of disappointment, however, that Cross dived into the world of gender equality.

After the 2008 election, Amy, who was working as a journalist at the time, decided to take an investigative look into the women who had made it into Congress. It was "a big year for women" as eleven democratic women got into Congress, and "I wanted to see how they managed to get there," Amy said. Amy worked with the Sunlight Foundation, an organization that tracks spending in politics, to figure out which industries fund which candidates. As a journalist, Amy wanted to see which industries helped fund the women that won that year. To her shock, she found there really weren't any. This was an "aha!" moment for Amy; she realized "the reason we don't have more women in government is because women are outside the funding mechanism." What women need, Cross realized, is to deploy more capital. "You vote with your dollar every day," Amy says, and if we take charge of our spending dollars, "women can get a lot done." By encouraging people who support women's leadership to "put their money where their mouth is" and shop Gender Fair, women can ultimately deploy more capital, become part of the funding mechanisms for politics, and see greater opportunity to be represented in government.

These examples show how technology has the power to not only unify people, but also provide tools needed to improve the health and well-being of people in many different ways. By pushing workplaces to create more inclusive and supportive spaces for women, apps like Woman Interrupted and Gender Fair are helping to create an environment that supports women professionals and women leaders. Being able to have your voice heard in meetings or have work policies that allow for better work/life balance allows women to take up space and recognize their value in their workplaces. This could not be any more important when it comes to helping women take their places as leaders in society; when you are surrounded by women leaders who you see are being supported and valued in the things they do, you are more likely to pursue positions of leadership as well. You are also more likely going to see other people recognizing the value women have in society and be therefore more willing to select them as leaders as well. In this way, the birth of these apps ultimately represents an era of progress and an overall change in thinking and perspective about women's roles and value in society, and when it comes to solving the problem of female unelectability, this is exactly the key ingredient we need!

CHAPTER 4:

ANTI-MISOGYNISTIC MEDIA, MARKETING, AND MOVIES

———

In addition to the creation of the Woman Interrupted app mentioned in the last chapter, Gal Barradas participates in women's leadership groups and invests in market, advertising, and technology-based startups with strong gender equality and diversity philosophies. Notably, she co-founded BETC São Paulo, a marketing and advertising agency with a cultural and operational agency model inspired by female empowerment, equality, and diversity. The BETC agency, with offices in Paris and London as well as São Paulo, has a 60:40 women to men ratio with four out of the seven people in top management being women. With a powerhouse of strong female voices on the team, the advertisements created by BETC have challenged sexism and misogyny in consumer markets with ad campaigns that promote and celebrate women and their value in society in ways that don't just appeal to their appearance, sexuality, or domestic capabilities. One of the most successful advertisements produced by BETC San Paolo is the #HerSheGallery campaign which transformed the packages of the well-known milk chocolate bar into a space to expose the work of female musicians, illustrators, poets, photographers, and other creatives for the month of International Women's Day.[53] BETC's 2020 Sephora ad campaign "The Unlimited Power of Beauty" encourages women to have a positive relationship with themselves and find confidence in the diverse and changing facets of their own, as well as others', beauty throughout their lifetimes.[54] The powerful ads highlight the marketing company's effort to champion gender diversity, a company vision which "could not be possible without the vision of the women working on those campaigns," says Barradas.

The marketing and advertising world isn't the only one making progress, however. The portrayal of women within magazines has also moved with the times and is taking much more of a lead on culturally relevant issues. Readers have a real appetite for issue-led content, and magazines have started to understand the issues their female-identifying audiences face. They have therefore been able to work out the most relevant, culturally important issues facing them—whether it's political or social issues, or the latest concerns around health, wealth, and beauty. *Teen Vogue,* for example, which has previously been known for its columns on fashion, beauty, and boy tips, has taken up the mantle on political debates for a younger audience. In its September 2016 issue, typically

53   "Hershey's: #HerSheGallery by BETC Sao Paulo" *The Drum*, accessed January 3, 2021.

54   "Ads We Like: Sephora Explores Changing Beauty Norms to Underscore Diversity Commitment," *The Drum,* accessed January 3, 2021.

the month in which fashion magazines focus on upcoming trends, *Teen Vogue* changed it up, featuring a personal essay by the presidential candidate Hillary Clinton, a conversation between the actor Amandla Stenberg with the feminist Gloria Steinem, and an interview with the US Attorney General Loretta Lynch, in addition to introducing "21 Under 21," the magazine's "official guide to the girls and femmes changing the world."[55] *Time Magazine* has joined in and made changes to their marketing, swapping out their seventy-two-year-old *Time* Man of the Year for *Time* Person of the Year, as well as creating their 100 Women of the Year project to spotlight influential women who have been overshadowed by their male counterparts but have changed and are changing the world as we know it.[56]

Movies, too, are seeing an improvement in the way in which they portray women. Following her 2015 speech for *Glamour*'s Woman of the Year Award, *Legally Blonde* star and founder of production company Pacific Standard Reese Witherspoon has been able to bring attention to the long history of sexism in Hollywood.[57] Witherspoon called for more complex, interesting female roles to be brought to the big screen and condemned the typecasting of women in movies as only bratty sisters, dutiful daughters, sidekicks, and sex symbols. Since then, box office success of female-led films have started to kick off. According to the study of

---

55 "Hillary Clinton Discusses Equality and Feminism with Teen Vogue's 2017 21 Under 21 Nominees" *Teen Vogue*, accessed January 17, 2021.

56 Kelly Conniff, "Behind the Scenes of TIME's 100 Women of the Year Issue" *Time*, March 5 2020.

57 Anna Moeslein, "104 Women Who Defined the Decade in Pop Culture" *Glamour*, December 20, 2019.

the top one hundred grossing domestic films of 2019, the percentage of films featuring a female protagonist increased to a recent historic high of 40 percent, up from 31 percent the previous year.[58] Characters like Katniss Everdeen from Lionsgate's *The Hunger Games* or Merida from Disney Pixar's *Brave* are changing the narrative of girlhood and challenging tired stereotypes by not waiting for some guy to save the day; the characters are saving themselves and their worlds, too. Katniss Everdeen is a cool, capable, focused heroine whose personal struggles for survival and dignity are joined to a larger fight for justice, and *Brave*'s Merida, Pixar's first female protagonist, competes for her own hand in marriage as part of a story line that centers on a positive mother-daughter relationship rather than a male-female one—a rarity for Disney princess movies. In this way, the picture of girlhood at the movies has become increasingly less misogynistic. Although the faces of these girls remain rather monochromatic (read blonde hair, blue eyes, and white skin), characters like Shuri (played by Letitia Wright) from *Black Panther*, lead actress Constance Wu in *Crazy Rich Asians,* and Priyanka Chopra in *Quantico* are certainly a good start as well. It seems as though representations of women present in the media are finally starting to become as diverse as women actually are in society.

I know when I see women in strong, lead positions in movies or read articles about what women achieve rather than what they look like, I feel more inspired to be a leader myself and I am sure I can't be alone in that feeling.

---

58 "Statistics: Facts to Know About Women in Hollywood" Women and Hollywood, accessed March 3, 2021.

So, while there is still a way to go when it comes to the diversity in representation of women on screen and in print, we have certainly come a long way in terms of our greater societal efforts to reduce stereotyping in our media, marketing, and movies. These changes are ultimately providing girls and women with different icons and female role models to look up to and relate to, allowing young girls and women to gain confidence and feel strong in themselves whichever way they portray their femininity. When girls and women see themselves represented equally, diversely, and positively on screens and in magazines, they are more likely to see themselves as important and valuable members of society and may therefore be more likely to see themselves in, and pursue, leadership positions.

As I noted in the earlier chapter "Only Woman at the Table," I believe there is "power in numbers," and as more women enter the male-dominated field of politics, the more likely it will be for other girls to explore politics as an option. Furthermore, because the media has so much power over the way society views women in leadership, positive representations of women in magazines, movies, and other marketing media can alter people's thoughts, choices, and actions in a way that narrows the gender leadership gap. In this way, the efforts by marketing agencies like BETC, magazines like *Forbes*, and movie production companies like Lionsgate and Disney Pixar are helping to change the way in which women are represented in leadership and are therefore part of the larger effort to support women leaders and make politics a more inclusive space for women.

Although the changes we are seeing in marketing, movies, and magazines are just one small puzzle piece in the ultimate solution for an equitable world, they definitely have the potential to encourage positive change.

CHAPTER 5:

#HASHTAG ACTIVISM

———

If you couldn't already tell by how often I reference them in this book, I'm a TED Talk enthusiast. Ever since we started watching them in my grade ten careers class, I was hooked. I particularly liked watching ones about feminism and gender issues; hearing women talk about the struggles they experienced and the ways in which those experiences showed them what needed to be changed in society inspired me. One of the first TED Talk videos I remember watching was Kristen Pressner's "Flip It To Test It" talk in 2016.[59]

In Pressner's TED Talk, she admitted she has a bias against women leaders. Even as a woman leader who works in HR where her entire job is about being unbiased, Pressner would find herself thinking about or treating women leaders differently. "Most of us have heard about unconscious bias" she said, "but deep down we all kind of think it's 'everybody else' who is the problem" instead of looking at how we all hold unconscious bias in ourselves because, well, we do. The

---

59   Kristen Pressner, *Are You Biased? I Am,* Filmed August 2016 at TEDx-Basel, Video.

antidote Pressner gives to this problem is to "mentally flip" the gender of the person in whichever situation you're in and "if it seems weird, check yourself." In other words, you need to "flip it to test it." Pressner's "flip it to test it" idea soon took to Twitter in the form of a hashtag. Starting in 2016, people started taking to Twitter to start conversations about unconscious bias using the hashtag #FlipItToTestIt. Still to this day, if you search the hashtag you will come across hundreds of posts of people sharing their #FlipItToTestIt stories and ideas. The hashtag became so successful, Pressner even had it trademarked!

The reason this hashtag works so well is because #FlipItToTestIt works unconscious bias by putting people in discovery mode, not defensive mode. By emphasizing unconscious bias is something we *all* struggle with, and by actually providing a way to deal with it instead of just pointing out it's bad, #FlipitToTestIt helps people to rewire their brains and challenge the stereotypes so deeply entrenched in our understandings of what it means to be a man, a woman, and a leader. What Pressner found is "if you send everyone to unconscious bias training, all you do is find everyone hates it...but if you find a way to get interest from a number of people and get people talking about this, it kind of takes on a life of its own." Sometimes, pushing and prodding at people to tell them to get rid of their unconscious bias will just make people feel bad about themselves rather than make them take positive steps toward making change. "I always prefer 'pull' versus 'push,'" Pressner says. The hashtag approach of #FlipItToTestIt does this.

Another example of a hashtag creating a more inclusive space for women leaders is the #BanBossy hashtag.[60] The hashtag is part of a self-censorship campaign launched in 2014 by Sheryl Sandberg's LeanIn.org. The campaign discusses how the use of the word "bossy" to describe assertive girls and women stigmatizes female leaders and may discourage girls and women from seeking positions of leadership. "We call girls bossy on the playground," Sandberg said. "We call them too aggressive or other B-words in the workplace. They're bossy as little girls, and then they're aggressive, political, shrill, and too ambitious as women."[61] Sheryl Sandberg expressed that she feels #BanBossy is needed to counteract the stereotype of girls being bossy; by challenging the use of the word bossy, #BanBossy encourages women and girls to raise their hand, speak up, and be a boss. "#BanBossy is for every little girl who's been called the B-word and held back as a result. This is for the next generation of [women] leaders and bosses," Sheryl says. The hashtag also blew up on Twitter; the hashtag #BanBossy has been used hundreds of thousands of times and has led to conversations in the news and between important decision makers about how gendered stereotypes affect women's leadership.

The #FlipItToTestIt and #BanBossy examples highlight just how effective hashtags are in generating change. The creation and use of hashtags for social change is part of what we now call hashtag activism. The concept of tagging social media groups or topics with a hashtag was birthed by a man named

---

60   "Ban Bossy. Encourage Girls to Lead" BanBossy, accessed January 3, 2021.

61   Cynthia McFadden and Jake Whitman, "Sheryl Sandberg Launches 'Ban Bossy' Campaign to Empower Girls to Lead" *ABC News,* March 10, 2014.

Chris Messina, who came up with the idea in 2007.[62] Medina got the idea of using a hashtag from online chat rooms and decided to pitch the idea to Twitter. At the time, Twitter told him it was "nerdy" and it would never catch on, but he did not give up. Instead, he started asking friends to give the hashtag a try, and eventually in 2009 it caught on. Now, millions of twitter users all over the world use it to get behind causes just like #FlipItToTestIt and #BanBossy.

Although many believe tweeting or posting information online is an effective form of advocacy, some critics have labelled the use of hashtags as "slacktivism," a lazy and performative kind of activism that doesn't actually create change. It is true the problem with activism on social media is that it is hard to know if the people engaging in it actually care or if it is just an identity performance played to be part of something that is trending, but it should be recognized Twitter hashtags play an important role in setting the scene and constructing an emotional space within which collective action can unfold. Because of the hashtag tool, movements like #NeverAgain, #MeToo, and #BlackLivesMatter movements have gained incredible momentum. We can't neglect the power hashtags have to share information and mobilize people behind a cause. At the end of the day, if we are trying to root out bias to create a more inclusive space for women leaders, hashtags might just be one of the best ways to do that.

<hr>

62   Erin Black, "Meet the Man Who 'invented' the #hashtag" *CNBC*, April 30, 2018.

CHAPTER 6:

THE POWER OF VULNERABILITY

———

"Learning is pain."—Brené Brown

Dr. Brené Brown is a research professor from Houston, Texas, whose work focuses on courage, shame, empathy, and vulnerability. She is best known for her TED Talk called *The Power of Vulnerability*, which has been viewed more than thirty-seven million times, in addition to publishing her best-selling book *Dare to Lead*.[63] In her interview on *Overheard* with Evan Smith, Brené talks about the state of sexism in our world today.[64] When asked about her thoughts on the progress we have made surrounding sexism (as well as racism), Brené reflected on something her therapist once told her: "Every great progression will require a massive regression before it happens." When asked by Evan Smith if Brené

---

63   Brené Brown, *The Power of Vulnerability*, Filmed June 2010 at TEDx-Houston, Video.

64   *"Dr. Brené Brown: Racism, Sexism, and Progress"* Overheard with Evan Smith, accessed August 2020.

thinks "today is the massive regression" Brené replied, saying "I do." Brené went on to say, however, she "holds on to this saying" as a reminder the pain we may be experiencing in the fight against sexism is a good thing because it means we are learning, and learning means progress.

For Brené Brown, the reason we are seeing progress is because we are finally learning the importance of being willing to "have hard conversations" and start "attending to the fears and feelings of others," especially when it comes to conversations about inclusivity, equity, and diversity. In her research, Brené has found experiencing vulnerability, shame, fear, and pain are a necessary part of the journey to becoming more fulfilled and whole-hearted people and are also, therefore, a necessary part of progress. She believes that, as a society, we are often hesitant to be vulnerable and tend to avoid conversations about the fears and feelings of others because it makes us uncomfortable, and we are afraid of what people are going to think. "Our culture encourages people, especially women, to be "nice" and "polite," and so people generally prefer to sidestep difficult situations." Brené notes that the problem with this is issues like sexism need to be brought to light and talked about if they are to be solved. Sidestepping those difficult conversations just allows the issue to continue, and you end up becoming resentful from having to "spend time playing whack-a-mole with people's bad behavior." What we need to do, Brené Brown says, is to "excavate and bring to surface and shine light on stuff people are feeling but not talking about."

Someone who is leading the way in opening up these conversations about inclusivity, equity, and diversity is Catherine

Clark, nationally recognized communications entrepreneur and daughter of former Canadian prime minister Joe Clark (as well as a fellow Elmwood School alumni of mine). After growing tired of having conversations with women who felt disempowered or unsupported in the workplace or were struggling to find balance between work and home life, Catherine Clark, along with co-founder Jennifer Stewart, decided to start a podcast titled *The Honest Talk*.[65] Through an "interactive, interview-style format" *The Honest Talk* hosts weekly episodes featuring inspiring female guests who have "excelled in a variety of sectors and who are committed to sharing their personal and professional experiences to benefit others." The show's guests discuss their motivations, concerns, objectives, experiences, and opinions to provide inspiration and advice for women to help improve or shape their lives. Catherine emphasizes that the show aims to include a wide array of different voices from diverse backgrounds so that all women will be able to listen and find something from the conversation that relates to them and their personal situation and "have their experiences, feelings and views represented" in the larger societal dialogue surrounding sexism. Through these conversations, the show works to provide a safe space for women to be open and vulnerable to have "real, deeply honest conversation about the experiences, challenges, aspirations, and lessons shared by women-entrepreneurs, business leaders, and up-and-coming female professionals."

Clark and Stewart had initially planned to do live events, but plans changed when COVID-19 hit, although not necessarily in a bad way. The switch to creating a podcast "has

---

65   "About The Honest Talk" The Honest Talk, accessed June 1, 2020.

been a great way to start out," Catherine says, and allows for a greater reach to women who live outside of the organization's base in Ottawa. Catherine notes that, especially in light of the pandemic, the pressures and struggles women experience, both at work and at home, "can leave women feeling quite isolated" and can "make them feel like they are the only one's failing to juggle all of their responsibilities as working women." The aspiration of *The Honest Talk* is to combat this feeling of isolation and "create a forum that leaves women feeling connected, inspired and motivated in their careers and personal lives." By giving women a chance to be vulnerable and honest with each other in a safe and supportive setting, women end up feeling less alone in their struggles. Moreover, the show relieves the stigma around female vulnerability, as the podcasts offer a greater awareness and understanding of the challenges faced by women and normalizes conversation about such issues. If you hear other stories of women who have achieved success saying, "'Yeah, I've felt tired, I've felt incapable, I've dealt with mental health issues, too,' that really helps to create solid footing for other women following behind," Catherine says.

The growing movement to accept and champion vulnerability, and talk with others about our individual and struggles, is an incredibly important one. Growing up in a very English, very stiff upper lip kind of family, my knowledge of what was considered strong was of stoicism and emotional coolness. Vulnerability was not part of the equation and personal struggles were seen as just that: personal and unaffiliated with others and other surroundings. It wasn't until I started studying some feminist theory in my communications classes during university that my notion of vulnerability started to change.

We studied Judith Butler's reconceptualization of human experience as relational and interdependent and of the inheritability of vulnerability in our state of being. Butler explains how we are exposed to and dependent on "infrastructure, understood complexly as environment, social relations, and networks of support and sustenance," and that vulnerability is affirmed in the way we necessarily affect and are affected through our interactions with one another. In this way, trying to dismiss vulnerability is like trying to dismiss the fact all of our actions have an effect on one another. If we dismiss vulnerability then we can't ever move forward; resistance and progress inevitably require acknowledgment that the way in which we act affects each other, and we need to change the way in which we act to effect change.

As Brené Brown would say, shows like *The Honest Talk* create "empowerment through empathy." When women open themselves up to being vulnerable with one another about the struggles, challenges, and experiences they face with sexism, women are not only able to take the weight off of their own chests and feel more empowered as an individual, but are also able to take the weight off the chest of society as a whole as well. The weight of the stigma, taboo, and distaste for uncomfortable conversations about sexism is pushed aside when people decide to say "screw being uncomfortable" and empathize with one another's perspectives and feelings. With that weight taken off, change-making conversation to be made.

PART 3

FIVE STEPS FOR A FUTURE WITH FEMALE LEADERS

INTRODUCTION

———

While it may be impossible to completely to rid our world of the barriers and bias against women leaders, we can combat them by working from the ground up, supporting women leaders by empowering each girl and woman as an individual to become strong leaders in their community. Leadership is a learnable skill, and it's also a muscle; the more often women practice being a leader and receive the support of the people around them to grow as one, the closer we will come to a brighter future for female leaders.

The upcoming section will explore some of the experiences I have found have helped me in my own journey of growing as a confident woman and leader in my own community, as well as other things I believe to be necessary or helpful in empowering women and creating a supportive environment for the growth of female leadership. The chapters in this third section will specifically take a look at the five steps we can take to empower women and girls and make the world we live in a more inclusive and supportive space for the growth of female leadership. These five steps are:

1. Conversation: about the way they think about gender equality, gender issues, and women in leadership and in politics
2. Education: to get people to learn about and reflect on gender bias and prejudice in society
3. Confidence: for girls and women to realize their abilities, intelligence, and capability of leadership
4. Action: by standing up for women calling out instances of gender discrimination, bias, and inequality
5. Accountability: of everyone, for everyone, to work on this issue and create change together

These steps and suggested actions may seem quite small, but they have a big impact. Change isn't just about big headline moments, legal victories, and international agreements. It's also about the way we talk, think, and act every day, and the ways in which little changes to these things can create a ripple effect that benefits everyone. As we usher in a new era of gender equality and commitment to supporting the growth of women as leaders in our day to day lives, I hope these five steps can provide some support and guidance to those who wish to partake in the process.

CHAPTER 1:

CONVERSATION

———

"We cannot change what we are not aware of, and once we are aware, we cannot help but change."

—SHERYL SANDBERG

"There is power in allowing yourself to be known and heard, in owning your own unique story, in using your authentic voice."

—MICHELLE OBAMA

In a 2019 TED Talk on "3 ways to lead tough unavoidable questions," Adar Cohen said something that really made me stop and think: "Any of life's transformative conversations are also the most difficult ones—those we tend to avoid—but we can't afford to avoid tough questions or conflict because without conflict, problems hide everywhere."[66] More simply put, if you want to make progress you have to talk about making it first.

———

66 Andar Cohen, *3 Ways to Lead Tough, Unavoidable Conversations,* Filmed October 2019 at TEDxKeene, Video.

As we discovered earlier in the book, women leaders often put up with behaviours that aren't a big deal when examined individually, but when repeated over time, they get old. It's hard to promote change if we aren't conscious of these behaviors and don't call them out. That is why we need conversation; awareness and getting comfortable talking about topics like this is the first step toward change. And yes, I get it. Talking about gender inequality and the bias women leaders face, especially in politics, is uncomfortable, but we can't solve the problem if people don't know what the problem is!

Think about the ways in which gender inequality is perpetuated. Formal structures like laws and policies certainly play a role. But everyday routine encounters between everyday people reinforce these roles—between friends and family, between husbands and wives, employers and employees, and candidates for office and the people determining their "electability." When enough of us are determined to be a voice for change, it sets the stage for broader transformation. To do this we need to learn to connect at a deep level with our community. This means stepping outside the comfort zone of having easy, surface-level conversations and instead allowing in-depth, honest, and meaningful conversations to be the norm.

Giving women, especially, the platform to discuss a topic that otherwise might be an elephant in the room is empowering for women and eye opening for men. We need to be open to have these "elephant in the room" conversations with family, friends, partners, and teachers, even if they make us or others uncomfortable. We need to give our peers permission to call out any attitudes or behaviors that could use a rethink, and we should encourage our peers to be willing to do the same for us. No one has all the answers, and often there's no one right way to handle any given situation, but by getting comfortable with the uncomfortable, listening with empathy, asking questions, and giving feedback, we will be able to create an environment primed for progress is what will get us there this openness and respectful critique will build stronger, trusting teams.

That being said, while being vulnerable and honest about your feelings is not only important, but necessary, it is important we describe reality without laying blame. We need to create more environments that allow people to feel comfortable enough to talk about uncomfortable topics in the first place, and that won't happen if people feel attacked and get defensive. Often people are afraid they are going to get shut down by others or say something others might find stupid, which discourages them from honestly expressing their thoughts and participating in change-making conversation. While it can be tempting to point fingers, change-making conversations explore issues *with* people, not *to* or *at* them. By doing this, hard conversations can happen without being hurtful.

Some of the best, most influential conversations I have had were the harder ones, the ones that were more personal or maybe resulted in a little more disagreement. Whenever I want to have an in-depth discussion about politics and social change, I go to my dad (yes, even when I want to discuss gender issues). Although we come from opposite genders, generations, and upbringings, and we definitely don't always see eye to eye, I find I learn the most from our discussions. Having someone with different perspectives than mine helps me to see things from a different point of view; it pushes me to think harder and more critically to reconcile my views with his (and sometimes persuade him mine are better!). My dad helps point out where my thinking needs some expansion, or where my arguments fall short, which ultimately helps me to learn and grow even more. It is this kind of open and honest debate that pushes us forward and helps us progress as a society. Instead of shutting out conversations that are hard or challenge our ideas, we need to be willing to have these kinds of conversations and grow together.

Whether it be on social media, in the classroom, or at the dining room table, participating in open and honest conversations about the way we think about gender equality, gender issues, and women in leadership and politics is a great way to help make change. Ultimately, the frontier for exponential growth in the area of gender equality and empowerment of women leaders is through human connectivity.

Recap:

- Encourage others to be vulnerable and to have an honest conversation about the way they think about gender equality, gender issues, and women in leadership and in politics.
- Ask the women in your life questions about the struggles, experiences, and issues they are experiencing and listen to what they say with empathy.
- Be open to having difficult or hard conversations with family, friends, partners, and teachers about ways to improve.

CHAPTER 2:

EDUCATION

———

"We have to attack cultural norms at the roots. The real impact every single person has in their hands is teaching children and all people around us on why gender equality is really important."

—ANDRÉE SIMON

"The ability to learn is the most important quality a leader can have."

—SHERYL SANDBERG

When it comes to creating a more inclusive environment for women leaders in politics, one of the biggest roadblocks is ingrained and entrenched norms and perceptions of what gender means. Unfortunately, as the earlier chapters have shown, our culture still tends to devalue the feminine and idolize the masculine. This is problematic for women and for men who are then restricted by gendered behavior expectations; under this system, men and women must police their behaviors to avoid ridicule, ostracism, or even violence. These restricted gender norms prevent boys from expressing feelings or vulnerability and discourage women from expressing strength and leadership aspirations. Ultimately, both men and women are held back. To help dispel these misguided viewpoints pertaining to gender, there needs to be a paradigm shift in how it is approached. If gender is perceived as a continuum rather than an either/or designation, what it means to be male or female becomes less beholden to toxic definitions. This change opens up a variety of opportunities for everyone.

Teachers, and others in positions of authority, have the power to create this change as they have a great deal of influence over the way people think, believe, and behave. Changing people's perceptions, attitudes, and behaviors surrounding the idea of women in political leadership is a complicated task, yet one of the most important tasks, when it comes to progress. By teaching others about how gender is less of a biological construct and more of a social construct, teachers have the ability to challenge the social conditionings that often expect children to conform to specific and limiting gender roles and expectations from a young age. Because feminism, sexism, and gender equality inform students' self-perception and knowledge, teachers should recognize the value of discussing them in the classroom and look toward ways in which they can encourage others to critically think about the gender norms and stereotypes they see around them.

A large part of my own learning has been influenced by one of my professors at university, Dr. Carrie Rentschler. Professor Rentschler is a scholar of Feminist Media Studies at McGill University, specializing in feminist media making, social movement activism, and political subjectivity. My first class with Professor Rentschler was a huge turning point for me in terms of galvanizing my interest and passion for gender equality and feminism. I am perhaps biased when I say Professor Rentschler is the best teacher in the world when it comes to learning about feminism. I have signed up for a course with her every semester since I first met her! I am grateful she has been able to provide me with new ideas and thinking about feminism during the writing of this book. In discussing this book with Professor Rentschler, we talked about how important courses like feminist media studies are for the progress of gender equality. Carrie Rentschler sees education as a "tool to create opportunity to challenge natural hierarchies." In this way, she reframes the idea of education and learning about "unlearning"; to learn is to critically think about what you know, why you know it, and what other knowledge there might be out there. Unlearning is an essential step to creating a more inclusive environment for women leaders; by rejecting old notions of gender and leadership, we can move forward and make space for new notions.

Another important factor in educating for gender equality, Professor Rentschler says, is "not just what you teach, but how you teach it." To get people to reflect on implicit bias and prejudice, you can't be in an environment of guilt and punishment. This encourages defensiveness and ultimately prevents people from being open to learning new perspectives. In our discussions, Professor Rentschler reflected on some difficult moments in classes with people who were apprehensive to reject old ways of thinking, but ultimately found the act of those students voicing their thoughts and concerns actually created a more critical and meaningful conversation, and therefore a better learning experience for the whole class. Because of this discovery, Professor Rentschler has attempted, in her classrooms, to create "conditions of co-learning" and a culture of everyone sharing knowledge rather than her imparting knowledge. She has found this is more helpful for progressive thinking and ultimately encourages people to do the work of learning.

When it comes to education, however, it should be noted learning is something that needs to be continuous and should be happening outside of the classroom just as much as inside. Having conversations, sharing ideas, stories, and resources are all part of the work of learning and unlearning. These processes are essential for changing people's perceptions, attitudes, and behaviors surrounding ideas of gender and leadership and will ultimately lead to a more inclusive environment for women leaders in politics.

Recap:

- Reflect on internal prejudice, assumptions, and bias about women in leadership.
- Engage in the process of unlearning.
- Think about how to learn and teach, as well as what to learn and teach.
- Create a positive and open learning environment that welcomes others to grow.
- Look for and share resources, initiatives, and events that encourage reflection on the issue of unelectability.

CHAPTER 3:

CONFIDENCE

"You gain strength, courage, and confidence by every experience in which you really stop to look fear in the face. You are able to say to yourself, 'I lived through this horror. I can take the next thing that comes along."

—ELEANOR ROOSEVELT

"I want every girl in the world to know that her voice can change the world."

—MALALA

Confidence is an essential ingredient in creating an environment that is supportive of women leaders. Confidence is the belief we can create a successful outcome through our actions. In other words, when we are confident, we believe we are good enough, we believe we have value to offer, and those beliefs are what lead us to take action. In light of all the stereotypes and double binds female leaders face, the ability to believe you are good enough and valuable enough to overcome the challenges that comes your way is significant.

This is why girls and women need confidence; women need to feel equal to be equal.

I found my confidence at Elmwood. My middle school and high school years at Elmwood School for Girls largely shaped my confidence and understanding of what female empowerment looks, feels, and sounds like. I was constantly surrounded by people who encouraged myself and my peers to pursue our career goals and passions and never thought I was less competent than my male counterparts or felt I wasn't suitable for a position because of my gender. I feel grateful for this confidence that has been instilled in me, as it has helped dispel some of the less encouraging narratives I have become increasingly exposed to throughout my working and university experiences.

What specifically impacted me was how much my teachers cared about my personal growth as an individual. It can be quite easy to feel like a number at school, so having a principal and a group of teachers who take the time to get to know you personally and who care about you as an individual, not just as a student, is empowering. Mr. Whitehouse, our school's vice principal at the time and one of my favorite teachers, would stand outside the entrance and welcome us back to school each new school year, greeting every single one of us by name. The fact he cared to take the time out to get to know all of the students made us feel special. My high school friends and I can look back at our experience at Elmwood and all agree Mr. Whitehouse made a difference in helping us feel like our thoughts and feelings were worth listening to.

As staff members at an all-girls school, my teachers understood and acknowledged the ways in which girls often need extra encouragement when it comes to confidence. In conversations with my teachers, we would check in about what was going on at home, how we are doing in our extracurriculars, or how we were feeling. I especially think back to the daily conversations I had with my homeroom teacher Ms. Chun about what I was excited or worried about, or the chats I had with my guidance counsellor Ms. Moffatt about my future goals and aspirations. I am still close with both of them today, and I consider them important members of my support network. I go to them both when I need advice and when I want to share good news because I know they are always in my corner. Ultimately, I think I gained the confidence I did because my whole person was cared for, not just my academics, and my teachers were a big part of being that care for me. Having spaces like this that support women's ambitions and makes space for them is key.

It is also important for girls and women to have female role models and mentors in their life who can provide them with motivation and inspiration to achieve goals and work through hardships. Women and girls need to see confidence, leadership, and accomplishment in other women to envision themselves with those qualities. Young girls need mentors who break free from stereotypes and model leadership, agency, and self-efficacy. Starting from a young age, we must embrace girls and their unique capabilities for what they are, not limit them by what society expects them to be. Girls must receive the message there are no limits to what subjects they can study, what careers they can pursue, or what futures they can obtain.

When girls and young women see strong female mentors and positive role models first in the classroom and in their school community, and later in the workplace, it can help better prepare them to tackle their future with confidence and imagination. It is helpful to expose girls early on to a diverse set of role models as consistently as possible. Strong role models can be women who are older, skilled athletes, coaches, community leaders, successful businesspeople, celebrities, politicians, religious leaders, confident peers, or any strong woman whose presence will resonate with the girls. Although there is power in showing girls women who are international heroines, power also comes from exposing them to people that are within that girl or woman's own life. My experience at Elmwood provided me with exactly that. Every single day I was surrounded by amazing female role models. I was lucky to be able to wake up, go to school, and spend time with so many inspiring girls and women as teachers, coaches, counsellors, and classmates, too.

As parents, teachers, friends, and partners, we need to support the women in our lives by encouraging women and supporting their confidence and belief in the value of their own views, skills, and leadership in order to reinforce the idea women do have something to contribute to society intellectually, not just as a daughter, wife, and mother. We should also be providing and encouraging women and girls to find other female role models to look up to. As they say, seeing is believing, and female role models are an incredibly effective way of encouraging women to see themselves as leaders as well.

Confidence can turn thoughts into action and goals into reality.

Recap:

- Provide girls and women with positive and supportive environments that encourage personal growth.
- Remind the women in your life of their intelligence and abilities and their capability of leadership.
- Provide girls and women with female role models. If you're a parent, guardian, or mentor of a young girl, help her find encouraging role models.
- Search for books and other media that positively portrays strong female characters in leadership roles.

CHAPTER 4:

ACTION

"Take care to get what you like or you will be forced to like what you get."

—GEORGE BARNARD SHAW

"I never dreamed about success, I worked for it."

—ESTÉE LAUDER

Although raising awareness of the challenges and discrimination women in politics face shows progress, talking alone will not stop the perpetuation of those forms of oppression. We also need action. It is necessary to stand with women and girls in their daily struggles for the eradication of patriarchal, sexist, and misogynist constructs so they may have access to equal freedom, equal respect, and equal power. Progress needs action, and luckily action comes in many forms!

From catcalling to mansplaining to inappropriate sexual jokes, women are faced with all kinds of sexist and disrespectful behaviors in public and private places on a daily basis. By taking action and being an active bystander by disrupting the status quo and challenging these ideas, we can make a difference. This means calling out any inappropriate behavior in a safe, respectful manner and asking questions to challenge the gendered prejudice and stereotypes that may have fueled such situations. This could come in the form standing up to strangers catcalling, talking to friends and family about upsetting behaviors, or writing to politicians, employers, advertisers, and media outlets who have referred to women and girls in a demeaning or unfair way. By standing up for yourself or for other women, you can set an example as to how women should and should not be treated, and by extension, help create a more supportive environment for women.

As I have attempted to do by writing this book, you can also share your ideas with others and encourage people to start reading, watching, listening, and learning more about the topic of gender equality. This could be done by starting discussions with your peers, sharing articles and videos, or even writing your own articles or making your own videos. For me, writing has been one of the best ways for me to share my thoughts with others, as well as just grow in my understanding of my own perspectives on gender equality. As I mentioned earlier in this book, my time spent as a staff writer at McGill University's *McGill Journal of Political Studies* has allowed me to write on topics surrounding gender equality and politics and share those thoughts with my friends, family, and the greater McGill community. By writing about gender issues and politics, I am taking action in creating the very progress I talk about wanting. In this way, writing helps me feel like I am actually making a difference; I feel my voice is important. Oftentimes, I think people forget just how much power their voice has; your stories, opinions, and perspectives matter, and they can affect change! Use them!

As we have discovered in this book, women remain woefully underrepresented in the highest political positions, but there is a way we can make a direct difference. That's right, we can vote! While candidates can ask us to vote for them, but we can also them questions like: What are they and their parties going to about gender equality? Are they planning to work hard to make Canada more gender equal? It is important to stay informed on upcoming elections and spread the word about strong women candidates and other candidates who champion gender equality. Register to vote if you haven't yet and check in with friends and family members to make sure they're registered, too. (It's the least you can do, given how hard women fought for suffrage.) If you're ready for a bigger commitment, join a political campaign full-time, encourage women you know to run for office, or launch your own campaign!

Another way to take action is to give up your time and resources and commit to an organization or group making change. For me, that was McGill Women in Leadership. By joining a team of other like-minded people who care about creating an inclusive environment for women, I have found more opportunities and ways to get involved and take action for gender equality. McGill Women in Leadership has allowed me to put my actions where my mouth is and be an active participant in events and initiatives that support women leaders in my community. Looking for groups like this in your close community can help you feel connected to a cause and see the difference you are making in your community.

Collective action can operate at every scale; nothing is too small! The first step is showing up. You could attend a town-hall meeting or a protest about a community issue or share an article or news story. If you can't find a group working on your issue, start one! There are so many causes you can get behind! To begin, pick a gender equality topic you care about and find a group or campaign devoted to it.

Recap:

- Call out instances of gender discrimination, bias, and inequality when you see it.
- Use your voice to share experiences, ideas, stories, events, and resources with others.
- Be politically informed and politically active and use your right to vote.
- Join organizations that support gender equality and give your time and resources to help their causes.

CHAPTER 5:

ACCOUNTABILITY

"If you see inequality as a 'they' problem or an 'unfortunate other' problem, that is a problem."

—KIMBERLÉ CRENSHAW

"Achieving gender equality requires the engagement of women and men, girls and boys. It is everyone's responsibility."

—BAN KI-MOON

Gender equality benefits everyone, and so does the representation and success of women leaders. If this is the case, why aren't we all stepping up to the challenge and fighting it together as a collective?

In the pursuit of achieving gender equality, the focus has often been on what is going on with women and girls— how to remove barriers for the inclusion of women, how to empower girls, how to ensure women and girls gain access to health, economic, educational, and other opportunities. All of these efforts are very important. However, since inequities are often created by unequal power dynamics between men and women, efforts that shift these dynamics, encourage behavior change, and engage men and boys as allies are needed for progress to happen. Specifically, the issue of underrepresentation or unelectability of women is often seen as a women's issue rather than a societal issue. This is a problem because we are all part of the system that disadvantages women, and it seems rather unfair to place the onus of fixing that entirely on women themselves. The fight for gender equality and inclusiveness in politics needs the voices and support of men, too. After all, as former Prime Minister Julia Gillard noted, "Gender equality is good for men too!"

Men have always played critical roles in the women's movement and today plenty of men are proud feminists. However, while some men have responded to the feminist movement in a positive and supportive way, others have been more apprehensive (some even antagonistic) about joining in. This is, of course, understandable. While I am a strong believer that men gain a huge advantage from feminism, let's face it: you can't make omelettes without cracking a few eggs. In this case, the eggs are the forms of power and privilege men have traditionally enjoyed; men now have to compete with more than just half of humanity for most jobs, are expected to do their fair share of domestic work, and can no longer use their power to obtain sex. These traditional beliefs and practices have a life of their own and a deep staying power, and feminism challenges it, which is undoubtedly an uncomfortable experience. However, it is absolutely necessary that men, as well as women, hop on board and support gender equality if we are to achieve it. At the end of the day, we won't be able to progress with a "men versus women" mindset; we need a "men *and* women versus sexism" mindset. Positive change can only happen if we work together.

It should be noted women, too, have been apprehensive about men's involvement. Some feminists have, at times, taken a hardline, separatist stance seeing the challenge of achieving gender equality as resting exclusively with women and ignoring men, their views, opinions, and ability to act. Instead of fighting for equality, some are fighting for all-female domination, which in itself defeats the ultimate purpose of feminism. This is foolish because we can't ignore men's own socialization within the very patriarchal system we are fighting to change. To fight for gender equality, we need to address everybody's role in it and work on reconfiguring gendered systems as well as changing our own personal prejudices and biases together. Women must also realize their rights are incumbent on the systematic partnership with men and on appreciating the specific needs and challenges young boys and men themselves are struggling with.

What needs to be understood is equality is relational. Gender inequality is rooted in uneven dynamics that give disproportionate power to one group versus another. Irrespective of the amount we invest in women, men also need to be willing participants in the redistribution of power between genders.

Having an intersectional lens is also important. Intersectionality has been a commonplace phrase in feminist rhetoric since Kimberlé Crenshaw coined it in the '80s.[67] Simply put, intersectionality is the notion the combination of different identity dimensions—race, class, sex, gender, position, age, sexuality—has a dramatic influence on the way we experience the world. This intersection of identities leads to distinct obstacles and/or privileges that those who share some but not all our identities may not experience. Too often when we are tasked with empowering women leaders, our efforts fall into the trap of a one-size-fits-all approach which creates a tradeoff: gains in simplicity mean sacrifices in efficacy. This trade-off particularly fails women who are doubly or triply marginalized, because—especially in Western workplaces—these efforts focus implicitly on solving for the challenges of white, middle-class, cisgender women as the default. The reality is that all women do not face the same issues and inequalities, and our efforts to make our world more inclusive for female leaders need to take account of this. The pursuit of gender equality must include social progress for other groups in society that have less power; this includes, but isn't limited to, those with disabilities, minority or indigenous groups, and the LGBTQIA+ community. Power comes in numbers, and so by ensuring gender equality initiatives involve all people as active and equal partners, we are more likely to have progress.

If we want a world that is more inclusive of women leaders, we all need to be part of the fight for it. We all need to hold ourselves accountable.

---

67   Katy Steinmetz, "She Coined the Term 'Intersectionality' Over 30 Years Ago. Here's What It Means to Her Today" *Time*, Accessed February 20, 2020.

Recap:

- Affirm the idea gender, equality, and ineluctability of women leaders is not a women's issue, but a social issue.
- Make sure conversations and environments are diverse and inclusive of everyone.
- Make a special effort to include the voices of those who are typically underrepresented in society.
- Encourage men to be part of the conversation and be active allies in fighting for gender equality.

FINAL WORDS

———

Writing this book was somewhat of a challenge. When it comes to analyzing the experiences of women in leadership, the fact of the matter is a whole lot of women have not actually been allowed to hold positions of political leadership, making for a rather small sample size for analysis. You may have noticed there is a lack of female politicians of color used as examples in this book. That is because the already small sample size of women in politics is significantly reduced when it intersects with sample size of people of color in politics. When I reflect on this problem, I ask: Why not a woman? Why not a person of color? Why not a woman of color? We know the capability and the skills are there, so why is the pipeline of female talent being cut short of positions of leadership?

As I have come to understand through my research for this book, it seems a change of status quo makes people uncomfortable; the society we live in still seems to be uncomfortable with the idea of women being in positions of power. As explored in the first part of the novel, the way we think, talk, and behave toward women leadership is shaped by our age-old biases and prejudices surrounding notions of masculinity and femininity. The conversations we see and hear are still wrought with misogynistic undertone, ones which see feminine traits as less desirable but also see women without feminine traits as less desirable. Women who fit the gender stereotype of traditional femininity are liked more but are not considered as leadership material, while women who reject those qualities in attempt to be considered leadership material are considered unfeminine and hence generally disliked. This way of thinking has left women in the "catch-22 situation" where women will be disliked no matter what women do, and has ultimately created a lack of "electability" or "likability" for women in politics. This problem of unelectability discourages women from pursuing leadership positions and holds women back when it comes to finding success in politics. However, this is something we can change.

In fact, it is something that already is changing. The fact that women are finally starting to be seen as important and capable leaders is a great sign of progress, and I believe it points toward a new age of inclusivity for female leaders. As explored in the second part, we are starting to see society actively try and change the way we think about and treat women in politics. This is evidenced by the effort many people, organizations, apps, and industries are putting into promoting gender equality and female leadership. The pushback against gender stereotypes and prejudices we see in apps like Woman Interrupted or podcasts like *The Honest Talk* are helping create a more inclusive space for a future of female leaders. I am hopeful this greater willingness of society to finally have open, honest, and vulnerable conversations about the struggles of women in political leadership positions will open up the doors for progress and change to be made and allow for the creation of an environment that is inclusive and supportive of female leaders. While the progress society at large is making is certainly encouraging, a great deal more work is left to be done, and we can do a lot of things as individuals to help. As explored in the third part of the book, we can also affect change by working from the ground up, supporting women leaders by taking actions individually to help empower girls and women to become strong leaders in their communities. I have been lucky enough to be surrounded by people that do just that; my friends, family members, teachers and colleagues alike have all had a significant impact on my own leadership journey, and through their individual actions have shown me how I too can help support a brighter future for women leaders through my own actions (and I hope writing this book will be a part of that).

I believe young women today have more reason to be optimistic about their future than any in any prior generations. As long as we continue to address and work on changing our beliefs and attitudes about gender and leadership, the future will be filled with female leaders and women will no longer be unelectable. I have great hope the women and girls of the future will be able to look at the world around them and see women are indeed electable.

ACKNOWLEDGMENTS

—

I want to say a big thank you to Professor Eric Koester for this opportunity, to all of my editors who have helped me along the way, and to New Degree Press for actually agreeing to publish my book! Thank you to my family for being my biggest fans and for always supporting me in my endeavors, especially to my dad who is my number one go-to when I need to talk over an idea or get feedback on my writing. Thank you to Elmwood School and to the Elmwood girls and staff who have been the most incredible support network for me, and to my new family at McGill Women in Leadership for all the encouragement and support. In particular, I owe a great deal of thanks to my best friend Eryn, who truly is the best friend a girl could ask for, and without whom I would not have been able to write this book let alone get through high school and university. Last, but certainly not least, I want to say thank you to Nic for always being there, for looking after me, and for keeping me well fed and hydrated during the writing process!

I would also like to acknowledge and thank everyone who committed to helping me publish this book by supporting my pre-sale. I wouldn't have been able to publish this book without you and I can't thank you all enough!

Eryn Lundrigan
Joelle Weinerman
Nicolas Lafreniere
Kylie Brownlee
Emily Bangsboll
Sheetza McGarry
Jen Walsh
Alison Whichelo
Gillian Whichelo
Fred Whichelo
Emily Grydziuszko
Jeffery Ball
Shelly Smith
Cabot Yu
Samantha Hood
Robert Haddow
Danielle Humilde
James Whitehouse
Gal Barradas
Katya Droznin
Elizabeth Murphy
Lily McRae
Lea Lepik
Maya Ladki
Jaime Dalby
Steve Page
Andrew Moore
Paula Maloney
Michelle LeBlanc
Emily Hartvich
Julia Demers
Eleanor Duffley

Felix Carty
Jenny Haddow
James Strawbridge
Jennifer Lafreniere
Cynthia Smith
Elizabeth Moloney
Brandon Baijnauth
Henry Richardson
Sarah Jackson
Pamela Hay
Sarah Kallai
Jamie Whichelo
Tara Preston
Katia Nadeau
Tess Buckley
Nelly Droznin
Maya Kors
Kiara Ayoub
Lawrence Moore
Johanna Dipple
Gulley Jodi
Franky Mercurio
Iryna Abramova
Donna Moffatt
Addie Naprawa
Neel Soman
Aileen Conway
Jessica Brandon-Jepp
Jean-Marc Lafreniere
Dana Belford
Megan Jenkinson
Catherine Clark

Cheryl Boughton
Gina Spiridaki
Matthew O'Connell
Erin Derbyshire
Ted Whichelo

Joan Sun
Heawon Chun
Janice Tubman Clarke
Candice Butler

APPENDIX

INTRODUCTION

"Coronavirus: How New Zealand Relied on Science and Empathy." *BBC News*, April 20, 2020.

"Facts and Figures: Women's Leadership and Political Participation" *UN Women*. accessed January 19, 2020.

Henley, Jon. "Female-Led Countries Handled Coronavirus Better, Study Suggests." *The Guardian*, August 18, 2020.

PART 1: THE GENDERED CATCH-22
INTRODUCTION

Heller, Joseph. *Catch-22: a novel.* (New York: The Modern library, 1961)

Vial, Andrea and Jaime L. Napier. "Unnecessary Frills: Communality as a Nice (But Expendable) Trait in Leaders." *Frontiers in Psychology* 9 (2018): 1866.

CHAPTER 1: IN-STYLE

"Masquerading as Miss Rankin" US House of Representatives: History, Art & Archives." 2017. accessed January 27, 2021.

"Facts and Figures: Women's Leadership and Political Participation" *UN Women.* accessed January 27, 2020.

Haraldsson, Amanda and Lena Wängnerud. "The Effect of Media Sexism on Women's Political Ambition: Evidence from a Worldwide Study." *Feminist Media Studies* 19, no. 4 (May 19, 2019): 525–41.

CHAPTER 2: THE PANTSUIT

Buchanan, Angela Marie. *The Extreme Makeover of Hillary (Rodham) Clinton.* (Washington, DC: Regnery Pub, 2007)

Clemente, Deirdre. "A President in a Pantsuit?" *APNews,* November 7, 2016

Clinton, Hillary Rodham. *What Happened.* (New York: Simon & Schuster, 2017)

Givhan, Robin. "Did You Notice Sarah Palin's Sweater? Good. You Were Supposed to." *The Washington Post.* January 20, 2016

Pozner, Jennifer. "Hot And Bothering: Media Treatment Of Sarah Palin." *NPR.org.* July 8, 2009

Tanabe, Karin. "Tim Gunn Still Hates Hillary Clinton's Pantsuits." POLITICO, July 8, 2011

CHAPTER 3: BAD MOM

Brockwell, Holly. "I Fought a Four-Year Battle with the NHS to Be Sterilised at 30—and Won." *Telegraph.* March 24, 2016

Domonoske, Camila. "New Zealand Political Leader Quizzed On Whether She'll Have Kids." *NPR.org.* August 2, 2017.

Graham-McLay, Charlotte. "New Zealand's Leader, Jacinda Ardern, Delivers a Baby Girl" *The New York Times.* June 21, 2018.

Hein, Tim "The 10 Most Publicised Abusive Comments about Julia Gillard," May 21, 2012.

Johnson, Edward. "Julia Gillard Fried Quail: Small Breasts, Huge Thighs: Australian PM Furious at Opposition Fundraiser Menu." *nationalpost.* June 12, 2013

Rourke, Alison. "Julia Gillard Poll Bounce Following Misogyny Speech" *The Guardian.* March 22, 2012

CHAPTER 4: CAN WOMEN REALLY HAVE IT ALL?

"Dads Who Share the Load Bolster Daughters' Aspirations." Association for Psychological Science—APS, accessed February 1, 2021.

Hay, Pamela. *Having It All by Not Doing It All: Goodbye Superwoman.* (Balboa Press, 2017) Kindle.

Slaughter, Anne-Marie. *Can We All "Have It All"?* Filmed June 2013 at TEDxGlobal. Video

CHAPTER 5: SHRILL

Balakrishnan, Anita. "Uber Board Member Who Helped Lead Sexism Investigation Joked That Uber's Female Board Members Talk Too Much." *CNBC.* June 13, 2017.

Bennett, Jessica. "What Do We Hear When Women Speak?" *The New York Times.* November 20, 2019.

Clinton, Hillary Rodham. *What Happened.* (New York: Simon & Schuster, 2017)

Deborah, James and Janice Drakich."Understanding gender differences in amount of talk: A critical review of research." Oxford University Press. (1993).

CHAPTER 6: LITTLE MISS BOSSY

Garrett, Rachel and Dominik Specula. "Subtle Sexism in Political Coverage Can Have a Real Impact on Candidates." Columbia Journalism Review (2018)

McGinn, Kathleen L. and Nicole Tempest. "Heidi Roizen." Harvard Business School Case 800-228. January (2000).

CHAPTER 7: HYSTERICAL

"The Double-Bind Dilemma for Women In Leadership: Damned If You Do, Doomed If You Don't" Catalyst, accessed December 2020.

Bellstrom, Kristen. "13% of Americans Think Women Are Less 'Emotionally Suited' to Politics Than Men." *Fortune.* April 16, 2019.

Brescoll, Victoria L, Erica Dawson, and Eric Luis Uhlmann. "Hard Won and Easily Lost The Fragile Status of Leaders in Gender-Stereotype-Incongruent Occupations." Psychological Science 21, no. 11 (2010): 1640–1642.

Fitzharris, Lindsey. "The Wandering Womb: Female Hysteria through the Ages." *Dr Lindsey Fitzharris* (blog). April 28, 2017, accessed January 3, 2021.

Jackson, Chris. "Nominating Woman or Minority Come Second to Nominating Candidate Who Can Beat Trump." *Ipsos* (2020).

Williams, Blair. "From Tightrope to Gendered Trope: A Comparative Study of the Print Mediation of Women Prime Ministers." PhD Thesis, College of Arts & Social Sciences, The Australian National University. (2020)

Winkler, Elizabeth. "Hillary Clinton's Charisma Deficit Is a Common Problem for Female Leaders." *Quartz*. September 11, 2016.

Yan, Holly. "Trump Draws Outrage after Megyn Kelly Remarks." *CNN Politics*. August 8, 2015.

CHAPTER 8: ONLY WOMAN AT THE TABLE
"Women in the Workplace," McKinsey, accessed February 11, 2021.

PART 2: CHANGING TIMES FOR FEMALE LEADERS
INTRODUCTION
Gambino, Lauren. "'I Won't Be the Last': Kamala Harris, First Woman Elected US Vice-President, Accepts Place in History." *The Guardian*. November 8, 2020.

CHAPTER 1: PANDEMIC POWER PLAYERS
"Daily vs. Total Confirmed COVID-19 Deaths per Million." Our World in Data, accessed February 11, 2021.

Henley, Jon. "'Complacent' UK Draws Global Criticism for Covid-19 Response." *The Guardian*, May 6, 2020.

Hollingsworth, Julia. "New Zealand Has Just Elected One of the Most Diverse Parliaments in the World. Here's How It Stacks up" *CNN*. November 16, 2020.

Taub, Amanda."Why Are Women-Led Nations Doing Better With Covid-19?" *The New York Times*. May 16, 2020

CHAPTER 2: ORGANIZATIONS MAKING CHANGE
"What We Do at She Should Run." She Should Run, accessed January 3, 2021.

"Susan Room Voice and Executive Coach." Susan Room, accessed January 3, 2021.

Wilkie, Christina."Here's What Kamala Harris Said at the Democratic National Convention." *CNBC*. August 19, 2020.

CHAPTER 3: APPS MAKING CHANGE

"Our Mission, Gender Fair." GenderFair, accessed December 3, 2021.

"Woman Interrupted." WomanInterruptedapp, accessed November 3, 2021

Barradas, Gal. *The Right to Finish Speaking* Filmed September 2017 at TEDxSaoPauloSalon. Video

CHAPTER 4: ANTI-MISOGYNISTIC MEDIA, MARKETING, AND MOVIES

"Ads We Like: Sephora Explores Changing Beauty Norms to Underscore Diversity Commitment " The Drum." Accessed January 3, 2021.

"Hershey's: #HerSheGallery by BETC Sao Paulo." The Drum. Accessed January 3, 2021.

"Hillary Clinton Discusses Equality and Feminism with Teen Vogue's 2017 21 Under 21 Nominees" Teen Vogue. Accessed January 17, 2021.

"Statistics: Facts to Know About Women in Hollywood." Women and Hollywood, accessed March 3, 2021.

Conniff, Kelly. "Behind the Scenes of TIME's 100 Women of the Year Issue." *Time*. March 5 2020.

Moeslein, Anna. "104 Women Who Defined the Decade in Pop Culture" *Glamour*. December 20, 2019.

CHAPTER 5: #HASHTAG ACTIVISM

"Ban Bossy. Encourage Girls to Lead." BanBossy, accessed January 3, 2021.

Black, Erin. "Meet the Man Who 'invented' the #hashtag." *CNBC.* April 30, 2018.

McFadden, Cynthia and Jake Whitman. "Sheryl Sandberg Launches 'Ban Bossy' Campaign to Empower Girls to Lead." *ABC News.* March 10, 2014

Pressner, Kristen. *Are You Biased? I Am* Filmed August 2016 at TEDxBasel. Video

CHAPTER 6: THE POWER OF VULNERABILITY

"About The Honest Talk." The Honest Talk, accessed June 1, 2020.

"*Dr. Brené Brown: Racism, Sexism, and Progress*" Overheard with Evan Smith, accessed August 2020.

Brown, Brené. *The Power of Vulnerability* Filmed June 2010 at TEDxHouston.Video.

PART 3: FIVE STEPS FOR A FUTURE WITH FEMALE LEADERS
CHAPTER 1: CONVERSATION

Cohen, Andar. *3 Ways to Lead Tough, Unavoidable Conversations.* Filmed October 2019 at TEDxKeene. Video

CHAPTER 5: ACCOUNTABILITY

Steinmetz, Katy. "She Coined the Term 'Intersectionality' Over 30 Years Ago. Here's What It Means to Her Today." *Time.* Accessed February 20, 2020.

Made in the USA
Monee, IL
29 May 2021

68975309R00089